The Boones singing "A New Song."

BOTTOM LEFT: I've always been in a singing family.
BOTTOM RIGHT: WLS Barndance Christmas Party—food for the poor and big smiles for Santa.

*TOP LEFT: Mama and
Daddy (Eva and Red Foley)
and 2 year old me.
TOP RIGHT: An old friend
recently sent me this faded
clipping.*

Sings With Her Daddy.

Four-year-old Shirley Lee Foley helps out her daddy, Red Foley,
on his morning program over WCKY. Mrs. Foley is at the right. Red
and Shirley Lee were singing "Little Sir Echo" when the cameraman
snapped the shutter. Each Saturday at 8:30 a. m. Foley is giving
talented young amateurs a radio break on his half-hour WCKY
broadcast.

TOP LEFT: One of my proudest moments—High School Homecoming Queen!
TOP CENTER: High School Student Council—Pat was President and I was Secretary.
TOP RIGHT: Some snaggletoothed carols for the Hollywood Press Golden Apple Christmas Party.

BOTTOM LEFT: Columbia University Graduation, 1958. Pat graduated with honors, 4 kids, and me.
BOTTOM CENTER: Arrival in California, 1958—turbulent years ahead!
BOTTOM RIGHT: Little Laury's debut—our fourth daughter in 3½ years!

TOP: *Flip Wilson gave the "new Boones" a roaring send-off on National TV.*
BOTTOM LEFT: *Comedian Jim Hampton and his wife Carol at a premier with the Boones... before*
RIGHT: *...after*

TOP LEFT: *Heidi has a ball during our poolside mail reviews.*
TOP RIGHT: *Lindy's our seamstress—and a good one! She made all three outfits in this picture.*
ABOVE: *Teamwork in the kitchen pays off for Mom.*

*RIGHT: The secret of
a happy family—
Taking time to talk
with Jesus.*

*BELOW: An
afternoon visit
with "some friends."*

ONE

WOMAN'S

LIBERATION

ONE WOMAN'S
LIBERATION

by

Shirley Boone

CREATION HOUSE
CAROL STREAM, ILLINOIS

ACKNOWLEDGMENT

Quotations are taken from **New American Standard Bible** by permission of Lockman Foundation, LaHabra, California.

FIRST EDITION, JULY, 1972

Library of Congress Catalogue Card Number: 72-81113

DEDICATION

To the memory of Eva and Red Foley, who gave me physical life and first love; and Betty, Julie, and Jenny.

To Pat, Cherry, Lindy, Debby and Laury, who have taught me more about real life and true love than I ever dreamed or hoped I'd know and experience in this life.

SPECIAL THANKS:

My deepest love and thanks to Nancy Anderson who believed I had something worth saying and not only encouraged me, but worked with me and helped me *say it!*

CONTENTS

PREFACE

Freedom! Liberation! Self-realization! Equality! Independence! . . . These words are flying thick and fast today, in flurries like snow. They please us, they excite us, they promise beauty and adventure and release of the human spirit—and then they melt away into the reality of day-to-day living, the compromise and tradition of gray existence.

Are these just words? Are they only ideas that are doomed, like snowflakes, to a temporary—almost imaginary—substance?

Women's liberation, gay liberation, black power, chicano power, old-age benefits, trade unions, lobbyists for everything—all these efforts are being made to insure fair treatment. Equal advantages and liberation of the individual to pursue his or her own destiny is the desired target.

I understand these efforts; I believe they're all asking good questions, seeking real answers.

All kinds of groups, formed because of their common interests and frustrations, are desperately looking for ways to guarantee their freedoms and be released from restriction—as groups!

You know what I found?

Freedom comes in individual packages.

And freedom isn't the absence of boundaries; it's the ability to operate successfully and happily *within* boundaries!

And sometimes these limitations are good friends in themselves! Dick Van Dyke said on a recent TV show, "Some men see the rules of marriage as a prison; others, the happy ones, see them as *boundary lines* that enclose all the things they hold dear."

I find myself in that second group, among the happy ones.

But before the happiness, there was heartbreak. Before the liberation, there was slavery—bondage of the worst kind: mental, spiritual and physical.

Please believe me, this book is not the naive "do-good" gushing of a pampered Pollyanna. It's the product of anguish, of disillusionment, of experimentation and defiance, of small gains and disastrous setbacks, of giddy happiness and soul-wrenching emptiness.

I'm the wife of a successful entertainer, the mother of four teenage daughters. I've traveled from plenty to poverty—to plenty again. I've known what it is to be anonymous and to feel neglected and deprived of any self-expressions; and I've been thrust into the TV spotlight before 80,000,000 people *in one week* and expected to perform!

I've been the "neglected housewife," the "forgotten woman," toiling in the kitchen, washing the same clothes and cooking the same meals year in and year out, raising kids and serving a husband—and being taken for granted. I grew up as "Red Foley's daughter," then became "Pat Boone's wife," and then "The Boone Girls' mother"!

I've wondered if my life had any meaning, if anybody would really miss me should I be gone, if I'd made the wrong choices and squandered my youth and my life—if I might not have had a glamorous career. I've wondered if there was such a thing as real liberation—for this one woman.

And thank God, there was—and is!

I want to share this glorious, individual freedom with you.

I couldn't have written this book four years ago, while I was lost in self-pity, buried in problems, chained with unwanted responsibilities. Many *do* these days, and the book stores are *flooded* with angry, frustrated, inflammatory volumes—written by angry, frustrated, empty women!

I feel so compassionate toward those women—because I've *been* there! But now the anger is turned to joy, the frustration to fulfillment, the emptiness to overflowing love and—liberty!

I know who I am, at last. *I'm Shirley Boone—a child of the King!* And I know who *you* can be!

Isn't it really *identity* we're looking for?

Look at the masses and the communication media these days. In movies and on TV almost anything goes if it gets a "laugh," or if it's done in the name of "art," or because it's "reality." Our emotions are being changed. Things that should shock us or at least concern us—don't. We're becoming apathetic. We need *guidelines.* We *need* direction and balance in this world instead of limitless extremes.

Man has come to feel he can solve his problems all by himself. But look what a mess we're making of things. This nation was founded under God and look how He blessed it. Originally, we were a humble people who leaned on Him. "In God we trust" was on our money and our nation prospered—now we trust the money more than God and it's *losing its value.*

We let the Supreme Court rather than the Supreme Being guide us on prayer in schools. We took *prayer* out—and *pot* replaced it.

The *family,* in healthy society, was an institution of love and order with the man under God, the woman submissive to man and the children obedient to parents. Then men decided they didn't *need* God, women decided they didn't need men and children decided they didn't need to respect authority. Now we're seeing the results: the broken homes all across this nation, a rootless "lost" generation. We're rapidly heading toward a 50% divorce rate nationally!

How do we get it all together again?

There's so much talk about *free love* these days. Well, what they're really talking about is free *sex*—and there's a big price tag attached to *that*: twisted emotions, unwanted children, V.D. epidemics, etc. The only *free love* around that I know about is described in John 3:16, "For God so loved the world that He *gave* His only begotten Son, that whosoever believes in Him should not perish, but have everlasting life!"

I used to think "everlasting life" started when I died! I was so wrong It's *now*—and abundant, *fulfilled* life! [1]

Does it sound suspiciously as if my recipe for liberation is linked somehow to the Bible? Well, it is! Obviously, all of us make *something* the basis for our decisions in life, our point of reference. I've suddenly found that *all* my answers are in the Bible. Some I've had to uncover through my own bitter experience, but the blueprint for happiness was there all along!

Let me illustrate it this way. Not long ago, Pat dropped his most expensive Swiss watch on the kitchen floor. It fractured into many pieces, which he disgustedly scraped up into an envelope. As he stood there shaking those pieces in the envelope, I realized that although Pat had all the ingredients, *only the manufacturer could put it back together and make it valuable again.*

Our lives are like that watch.

So many of us are fragmented, rusted, displaced, disoriented, even shattered and with vital parts missing. *We need to return ourselves to the Manufacturer!*

And the Manufacturer's Handbook (as Pat calls the Bible) tells us how to do that.

Recently someone, remembering our old, strict adherence to unwritten but rigid doctrine, asked, "Pat, when did you and Shirley get so liberal?"

Pat laughed at the question.

"We didn't get liberal," he said. "We got *literal!* As soon as we learned to take the Bible literally, we found a whole new, happy way of life."

God is *sovereign!* He made us—and He deals with us individually!

I'm convinced that *submission* is the key to freedom in Christ, and that the *balance* of the Word and the Spirit will bring victory in Jesus.

I know there's so much more I need to learn, and as I learn more truth, it will erase error in my beliefs. The experiences in this book are shared in love, with my spiritual understanding at a new level. I pray that I will cause no one to stumble, but challenge you to study the Word of God. It's the key to your liberation!

My purpose in writing this book is to share with you what God has done for me—not to limit you to my experience, but to open you up to seek more of Jesus in your life.

I in no way want to over-emphasize the *gifts* of the Holy Spirit, realizing as Paul teaches: "Though I speak with the tongues of men and of angels, and have not *love*, I am become as sounding brass, or a tinkling cymbal. And though I have the gift of prophecy, and understand all mysteries, and all knowledge; and though I have all faith, so that I could remove mountains, and have not *love*, I am nothing. And though I bestow all my goods to feed the poor, and though I give my body to be burned, and have not *love*, it profiteth me nothing." I only want to open you to the validity of the gifts—when and if they help you glorify Jesus!

What a glorious individual liberty there is in God's "forever family!" As Jesus, my Savior and my Messiah says, "If the Son therefore shall make you free—you shall be free indeed!"

1
Runaway

"Pat, Cherry's gone!"

I didn't scream and I didn't audibly sob. But as I handed my husband the note which said our oldest daughter had left, I was inwardly fighting the panic of every mother whose child has disappeared.

Fifteen years old—and gone! She seemed such a baby, and she had run away from home.

Cherry's flight, it seems to me, is a good place to begin my story, because it provided one of the most painful tests I've ever endured. And, perhaps as much as anything Pat and I have experienced in the years of our marriage, it brought the two of us, together, into extreme closeness with God. The two days our daughter was missing from home gave us a deeper understanding of God's love by showing us how wonderfully He works when we rely on Him.

In Pat's book, *A New Song,* he has told how each member of our family came into a close relationship with God through being filled with the Holy Spirit, ending several years of weakening religious faith and deteriorating love for each other.

We had reached a point of bleak hopelessness when God, through the Holy Spirit, blessed us with a new faith and joy beyond anything we had imagined possible. Through surrendering to Him, we received what the Bible calls "the peace which passeth understanding."

Did this mean all our problems were gone forever? Of course not. In fact, some new ones were just beginning!

We'd just come home from a terrific vacation in Hawaii. Pat, the girls and I had loafed and played together, enjoying ourselves as a family, and we'd also found time for some serious talks which, I felt, had done us all a great deal of good.

It's often easier to talk about communicating with your children than it is to *do* it, but while we'd rested and played in Hawaii I felt reassured that we'd also communicated.

Although the day after we got home was a school day, I'd told the girls that they could sleep late for one morning and miss classes while they adjusted to the time change.

So, when Cherry didn't come down to breakfast, not even a late breakfast, I didn't think anything about it at first. In fact, I didn't even realize something was drastically wrong when I first noticed that *a car was gone.*

Suddenly, though, my mind did a double take and it dawned on me: Cherry was the only one other than Pat and I who could drive. A car was gone—she hadn't come to breakfast—so—

I dashed upstairs to her room, though even then it never occurred to me that she might have run away. Other girls ran away. Certainly they did. But not one of *our* daughters. The idea that Cherry might have been gone for more than an hour was simply too incredible to enter my mind.

Why, she only had a learner's permit, and I was both alarmed and hurt to think that she'd do something as wrong as to take a car out by herself—even for a few minutes!

14

But when I opened the door to her room, my heart jumped and, for the space of a breath, it seemed to hesitate as I looked at Cherry's neatly made bed with a note on it and realized that she *hadn't slept at home.*

I think I was still reading her note, numbly trying to digest it, when I called Pat and heard him running up the stairs.

Cherry's note clearly said that she would be back in two days, on Tuesday night; that she was going because she needed "to be alone with God," and that we shouldn't worry. All very calm and matter of fact.

But all I could think, in the instant of initial shock, was, "Oh, my baby. She's only a baby!"

Then, almost as quickly, I prayed, "Dear God, please protect her. Dear God, please help the rest of us too."

Pat was beside me now, and instinctively we began to pray together. If God weren't with us now, nothing could help. Without His protecting love, Cherry might already have become a victim of—

Thoughts too dreadful to define insistently pushed their way into my prayers.

Our beautiful, innocent, little girl had taken her *sleeping bag*! She'd said so in her note. I could just see her trying to sleep beside some lonely roadway, attractive prey to drug addicts, sex maniacs, the most depraved fugitives from society.

Since she had written that she wanted to be alone with God, Cherry would certainly have gone to a lonely place, I thought, where, unless God sheltered her, the most unspeakable horrors could overcome her.

As a child I had lived in Chicago where, during my childhood, a girl had been murdered in a particularly brutal way. Adults discussing the crime had filled my young mind with horrors which haunted me for years. Now as I prayed for Cherry, they flooded back, causing me sudden nausea.

"What should we do? Shall we call the police?" I asked Pat who faced me across Cherry's touching, näive note.

"Let's think a minute, honey,' he said.

After a moment of silence, I felt I knew.

The fact that she had gone away with her sleeping bag, completely oblivious to danger—her confidence that God would be with her—was so intensely moving that it gave us an answer to my questions.

"Nothing except pray," I said. And before Pat spoke again, I knew he was in complete agreement.

A year or so earlier, if I had been confronted with such a crisis, I would have called the police, jumped into the car to carry out a frantic search of my own or, almost certainly, have grown so hysterical that they'd have popped some pills into me and put me away.

Worst of all, Pat and I might have been yelling at each other, each blaming the other for the failure which had driven Cherry away. But now, thanks to God, we made no predictable human mistakes.

How the devil was twisting the screws though!

Cherry couldn't have picked a worse time to leave, for the morning newspaper had carried a story about a lunatic still at large who had been senselessly attacking campers. *Shooting at them!* I'd just finished reading that story when I went upstairs and found Cherry's note, so you can just imagine this frantic mother.

And, yes—yes, of course—I was frantic. So was Pat. Yet we were so certain of the overruling power of God that we avoided mistakes which would have made matters worse.

We realized instinctively what the headlines, "Pat Boone's Daughter Disappears" could do to all of us. If Cherry were in danger, the danger could be deepened by her public identification as Pat's daughter.

Since she'd promised in her note that she'd be home Tuesday night, an all-points bulletin for her apprehension and return would convince her that we had no confidence in her. But, as the ultimate tragedy, it would convince her too that we had no confidence in God. If *she* could entrust her safety to God, she'd wonder why Pat and I couldn't do the same. All our talk about faith, she'd almost certainly feel, had been only pious hypocrisy.

So we didn't call the police. Alone, together, and with our other daughters, we prayed to God, while He in His mercy gave us the strength to survive quietly the next thirty-six hours.

I could understand why a girl leaves home in anger, because when I was about fifteen (the age Cherry was when she left) *I* had run away too!

I thought of that when I saw Cherry's note. It was almost as though God were teaching me what I'd put my parents through—as though He were proving to me that the bread you cast on the waters will surely come back.

But there was a difference in the two incidents. I ran away in fear and anger. I'd been disrespectful to my mother and was afraid of what my daddy would say, so I'd lifted a screen off the window in my room, slipped out, and gone to my girl friend's house.

As soon as I'd left, I'd wanted to turn around and go home, but I was afraid to. Even so, I was back the same day.

Cherry's thinking when she left home wasn't at all like mine had been. Naturally she and I had had occasional misunderstandings. I doubt that there has been a mother-daughter combination in the history of the world who hasn't. But there had never been a serious rift between Cherry and me or between Cherry and Pat.

At fifteen, she wasn't allowed to go out alone with a date. Although she had a boyfriend (who happened to be nineteen), he came to our house to see her. The fact that she couldn't go out with John had caused some problems between them, but Cherry had tried very hard to understand

17

our decision in the matter.

Pat had told them, "I trust you two; it's old human nature I'm suspicious of! You'll have to wait till Cherry's a little older."

When there was a party or some event at school, Pat would take Cherry and John over and back which, when you consider today's standards, does sound peculiar. However, Cherry didn't protest the rules we laid down. She even seemed to appreciate them, because, since John *was* so much older than she, she realized that she might find herself in situations she wasn't equipped to handle if she were free to go and come as she pleased.

Cherry at fifteen was trying to determine just what her relationship with boys should be and, for that matter, just how to relate to the human race! Life, you know, can be very confusing to a young person who is sensitive and intelligent but so very inexperienced.

To add to her emotional burdens, Cherry had recently lost her best friend, Wendy, a lovely girl who'd died suddenly. And, while her religious experience was a great consolation, it sometimes added to her confusion. Cherry had to be sure that her faith was true and her own, not just a patchwork of dogma based on the experience of others and draped over her like a secondhand cloak of uncertain fit.

So, without understanding in the least how much she was going to hurt us, she had decided, "I don't want other people telling me what God wants me to do. I have to go out, be alone with Him, and find out for myself what He expects of me. I want to hear His voice."

The note Cherry had left for Pat and me was so loving—in no way rebellious or hostile.

It told us in effect, "Don't worry. I'll be fine. I'm taking my sleeping bag, and I'll sleep in the car with the doors locked. I love you so much. Please don't worry about me. I'll be home Tuesday night."

She even told us when she would be home! Nevertheless,

you can imagine what a terrible time of testing the following hours were for Pat and me.

Finally we did call my sisters and the George Otises, close family friends, because all of these are people of great faith who can call down God's power. After that, we could only pray.

Of all the things Pat and I have faced together, the most difficult (for me at least) was to trust God with my firstborn child. From time to time I couldn't help imagining Cherry in an automobile accident, trapped maybe under a car that had rolled down a canyon, or in the hands of madmen or killers.

Then I'd remember how God had protected Joseph when he was thrown into the pit and later when he was sold into Egypt. And, as I prayed, a peace so comforting that it can't be described in earthly terms would sustain me. I *knew* that a guardian angel was protecting my child. I can't explain how I knew, but I did! The Holy Spirit seemed to reassure me, "God isn't through with this child. He has more plans for Cherry."

From time to time, though, since I am human, my fears would return. I'd imagine Cherry vulnerable on the beach or on a mountain road, trying to be alone with God, but attracting the attention of perverts and sadists.

When these negative thoughts intruded, I'd get on my knees and beg, "Jesus, take such thinking from me." And I'd rebuke Satan in the name of Jesus, for I knew the devil was tempting me to doubt the power of God. Once, in real agony, I prayed that my own guardian angel would be taken from me and sent to protect Cherry. I was weeping, I think, and not even conscious of my words. I was simply opening my heart to the Lord. But the other girls heard me and, months later when Laury told Cherry about my prayer, Cherry cried.

Oddly, while Pat and I were sometimes distraught and fearful, our other daughters, Lindy, Debby, and Laury, were perfectly calm. We'd all received the Holy Spirit before that time, and the girls had more calm confidence—more certainty that Cherry was safe—than Pat and I.

By Tuesday evening I'd been tested almost beyond my endurance. At a quarter of ten I'd been drained, so I fell to my knees and told the Lord, "You've promised that You won't give us more than we can bear. Well, Lord, I can't bear very much more, so please send Cherry home. I'm trusting You not to ask much more of me."

I'd no sooner risen from my knees and walked downstairs than I saw the lights of a car turning into the drive! God had answered my prayers and kept Cherry safe. She was home!

Poor Cherry. She'd never realized what effect her disappearance would have on her parents. She'd only done as all of us do sometimes—acted on impulse without considering carefully all the consequences.

And when she did understand how grieved and frightened we'd been, she cried. Since she'd spent the past two nights in front of the homes of friends, she'd felt entirely safe. And she was horrified to discover how she'd tortured her parents.

Nevertheless, Pat and I knew that Cherry had to be disciplined for her thoughtlessness, because even though she hadn't *intended* to hurt us, she had taken a car before she had a driver's license, and she had left overnight without permission.

For punishment, she was denied her driver's license—something she wanted badly—for another six months. Cherry was disappointed, of course, but she accepted the discipline without argument since she knew that she deserved it.

That was more than *I* would have done at her age. For, when I was Cherry's age, I knew less than she did about a personal relationship with Jesus.

2

Born To Live

If you don't like to tap dance in public, it's tough being named after Shirley Temple.

But that's where I got my name, from adorable, dimpled Shirley who could sing and dance and act and who had nice, bouncy, sausage-shaped curls.

I came from a talented show-business family, but whether I had talent or not was a mystery I worked hard to preserve. Mom and Daddy tried to teach me "cute" songs, and I learned a few; but I remained a normal, gangly kid whose insecurities deepened every time I compared myself to America's favorite moppet, the dimpled, lively darling of "The Good Ship Lollipop."

Mama, hardly more than a child herself when I was born, dressed me like a doll and carefully coiled my reluctant hair into numerous sausage-shaped ringlets. However, I offset the effect by being a tomboy.

My mother was only fifteen years old when she married my daddy, a twenty-one-year-old widower with a daughter.

The responsibilities of being a stepmother as well as a wife at only fifteen must have been awesome for Mom! I can't imagine one of my daughters at fifteen—or myself either for that matter—coping with the obligations she accepted.

She'd grown up with a religious background, for her parents were members of the Salvation Army. Mother was part of a trio called "The Three Little Maids" singing at radio station WLS in Chicago when she met my father, Red Foley.

If you remember my daddy, as many of you must, you know he was a gifted Country-Western musician and singer with such a warm, outgoing personality that everybody liked him. He was basically a good man, with a tender childlike heart. His first wife had died when my half sister, Betty, was born, so he must have fallen head over heels in love with my mother to have married for a second time while he still had his career to build and a little girl to support.

We lived in Chicago until I was twelve years old, and while we were there I didn't really understand that Daddy was a celebrity. I *do* remember that he received some crackpot notes, even kidnap threats, and that the FBI came to our house; but, at the time, I don't believe I associated all of this with Daddy's work.

So far as I was concerned, when I was very small, he just had a job like other children's fathers. Not until I was much older did I realize that he was an important entertainer. Then I came to the horrible conclusion that people might be friendly to me only because I was Red Foley's daughter.

On the other hand, the threats and the FBI did frighten me and make me more insecure. Obviously I was a mixed-up kid, already developing into a budding runaway.

One day while I was in an alley bouncing a tennis ball against a garage door, something happened which shocked me so much I didn't get over it for a long time. An old car stopped near where I was playing, and the driver called to me. Thinking he wanted directions to some place in the neighborhood, I ran over and hopped up on the running board.

Coming from an all-girl family (I had three sisters), I'd never seen a nude male. Not even a baby! So I was horribly shocked when I innocently looked in the car window and saw that the man was exposing himself! Fortunately I was too stunned to see much of anything, but I was scared to death.

I ran to the nearest neighbor's house, crying and trembling and too frightened to speak. The neighbor walked me home to where Daddy was digging in our victory garden with a pitchfork. When he saw me shaking and crying, he tried to find out what had happened. But, because of the atmosphere in our home, I was too modest to tell him.

Finally, through questioning and by a process of elimination, Daddy guessed, and I had to admit he was right. I don't know what horror he felt at that moment; but when Daddy knew what happened, he grabbed his pitchfork and ran for the alley! And I was more afraid when I saw him go than I'd been when I stood on that running board.

My daddy, I realized, might *kill* somebody, and the thought terrified me. I don't know what would have happened if the man had still been in the alley—whether Daddy could have contained his anger or whether the instincts of an enraged father protecting his little girl would have led to an awful tragedy. But I remember I was more afraid of what my father might do than I'd been of that man! The man was gone, of course, and I've often thanked God for the time lapse which allowed him to escape.

If I'd been a different type of child, less modest and more outspoken, the episode might have had an irrevocably horrible conclusion. It might have destroyed a father I very much loved.

As time passed and the police and FBI asked me questions, I rather began to enjoy the attention I was receiving. There'd been several cases of indecent exposure in Chicago at about that time, so I was questioned in detail and even asked to try to identify suspects. However, I couldn't even identify the car the man had been driving— much less the man himself. Though the attention was exciting for a time, it didn't erase other effects of the incident. Small, nerve-wrenching experiences do take their toll.

Meanwhile my mother had become ill. I didn't understand *how* sick she was until after we left Chicago. She had developed a heart condition which, at that time, couldn't be corrected, even though she became one of the first to undergo open-heart surgery.

Unless a person is in bed with a doctor in attendance and medicine on the bedside table, it's hard for a child to believe that the person is seriously sick. During much of her illness, my mother was up and about and seemed well enough as far as I could see. However, when she'd lapse into unconsciousness, or begin to bleed from her nose or mouth if she were walking uphill, I'd be terrified. Sometimes I'd be horribly afraid that she was going to die. While at other times, when she must also have been in great physical distress, I didn't know that she was sick at all.

When I was about ten years old, Mom was ordered to bed for thirty days. This convinced me that something terrible was going to happen to her. Later, when she got up again, I forgot to be afraid. However, those thirty critical days made a lasting impression on me.

On the other hand, another relative, my aunt, became gravely ill, and her illness indelibly marked my life. Not only did it lead me to try to make a bargain with God; it resulted in my baptism.

While my parents had come from religious backgrounds (my father had been reared as a Baptist) and they had planted seeds in my heart that made God very real to me, they didn't take or even send me to Sunday school when I was small. But, somehow on my own, I had gravitated to a

Baptist church just down the street from my house.

I'd sensed the nearness of God always, in the change of seasons and the flights of butterflies, in the natural beauties all children instinctively respond to. However, I'd never thrown myself completely on His mercy nor presumed to make any major requests of the Father I still knew rather casually.

Nevertheless, when my "Aunt" Connie—my friend and playmate who was only nineteen days older than I—lay near death, I not only turned to God, but I also made Him an offer.

Connie's appendix had ruptured, and her condition was critical. I realized this from overhearing adult conversation, and I was desolate. What, I frantically wondered, could I do to help the companion I so dearly loved?

At the Baptist Sunday school I'd been attending, I'd heard stories of the miracles performed by Jesus, His disciples, and the prophets. Remembering these, I knew that God could save Connie. Of course, *that* was the answer! Even though Connie's doctor lost heart, *God* could make her well. I was sure He could, if only He *would*.

Since I was a child with my faith unhampered by sophisticated notions and world-weariness, I prayed in the pure and perfect belief that God would hear. As I prayed, I tried to form a pact with a faraway, unimaginable God, speaking to Him as openly as I spoke to my earthly daddy.

"If You'll let Connie live," I promised, "I will serve You the rest of my life. Dear God, I really will."

Mine was a sincere promise made by a child who didn't know how difficult God's service sometimes can be, or, to reverse the coin, how gloriously rewarding. However, God heard me.

In the ensuing years, I haven't always kept my pledge; yet, I've never forgotten it. And on the occasions when I've failed God most shamefully, the memory of a ten-year-old's unblemished faith has intensified my sense of guilt. If only each of us could trust God as completely as I did when I was ten and asked for my aunt's life, how easily our problems would be solved!

Connie lived; and, still feeling very close to God, I decided to be baptized. My mom and dad came to the baptismal service, and I remember asking my Sunday school teacher to sit with them if she could.

The decision to be baptized was entirely my own and very important to me. Although I was only ten, I thought of baptism as something extremely personal and important—something just between me and Jesus. I didn't even feel that I was being baptized into a church, but rather, into Him.

Shortly after this we learned how sick Mom was, and during the next few years I needed God a lot. Mom died when I was seventeen, but from the time I was ten until the time of her death, her health profoundly affected our family life and emotions.

Looking back, I sometimes think I lived in constant fear that she was dying. This wasn't really true, though, because on her good days I'd wonder whether she was even ill. Then she'd be worse, and I'd feel horribly guilty and more scared than ever because I had doubted.

When I was twelve, our family moved to Nashville, ending one chapter of my life and beginning another which, in outline, sounds like a soap-opera script.

For in Nashville, I discovered I was the daughter of a star.

I lost my mother.

And I found Pat Boone.

3
The Ugly Duckling

"Yankee, Yankee, Yankee! Shirley is a Yankee! Just listen to how a Yankee talks!"

I'd never been called a dirty name before, and, for that matter, I'd never before thought of the word *Yankee* as dirty. In Chicago it was part of the title of a patriotic song, "Yankee Doodle," and an adjective that meant something *good*—as in the phrases "Yankee know-how" and "Yankee thrift."

But among neighborhood kids and my classmates at Woodmont School in Nashville, Tennessee, the word *Yankee* was definitely a verbal mud ball and usually a noun—as in the phrase "damn Yankee." No, the children didn't say *damn,* but the very word *Yankee* as spoken by the kids at school sounded scornfully profane.

It's hard for a twelve-year-old child to be uprooted under any circumstances because of the physical changes going on at that age when she is unduly awkward, overly sensitive, and easily driven to tears. Also, at twelve, children are more clannish than individualistic. They join clubs, go to spend-the-night parties and, above all, want to do whatever it is that "everybody else" is doing.

So, for me to leave my friends and classmates in Chicago and move to a strange town called Nashville was a large enough jolt. But to discover myself not only a stranger but a "foreigner" at Woodmont School was horrible.

Nashville is an old city, built so solidly around families which have been there since the eighteenth century that the past there often seems quite current. Descendants of Charles Dickinson, killed by Andrew Jackson in a duel, and descendants of John Overton (who was Andrew Jackson's close friend and law partner) don't let their families' past differences interfere with their present social life, but each Nashvillian of old lineage has a strong sense of history and of what his or her family has contributed to the town. Not only do friendships go back for generations, but kinships through blood, marriage or courtesy abound.

The society folks of Nashville don't intend to be snobbish. For the most part, they are kind and well mannered. Nevertheless, because social circles have been complete there for so many years, it's hard for a stranger to become a genuine part of the city—especially if the stranger is a Yankee!

Three small anecdotes may explain what I'm talking about:

An older woman, in conversation with a friend of mine, said, "When I was a young girl, and a young man came to call on me, the first thing my father asked him was, 'Who was your daddy?'

"Then he'd ask, 'And who was his daddy?' Then, 'Who was his daddy?'

"Then he'd say, 'All right. Sit down.' "

In the same vein, a younger woman who was active with the Tennessee Walking Horse Association remarked, "Of *course* I'm interested in family histories. If a blood line can tell you how a horse will probably perform, why shouldn't it tell you the same thing about a person?"

Undoubtedly there is a strong correlation between the passion for horse breeding, which produced the famous Tennessee Walkers, and a preoccupation with human genealogy.

Finally, an elderly widow born in another state but a resident of the area for fifty years was active in social and civic affairs and, to all outward appearances, was an integral part of the community. However, after an argument with one of her close friends about some civic matter, the widow conceded the match when the friend said, "But you can't possibly understand this, Sarah. After all, you are a newcomer!" And with that winning point, wiping out fifty years' residence, she closed the case.

Of course, not everybody in Nashville has been there forever. The Grand Ole Opry group, of which we Foleys were a part, draws many *new* people to the city. But, as a twelve-year-old, I wasn't part of the Grand Ole Opry crowd either, partly because my parents didn't encourage me to be. They, quite rightly, wanted me to have a life that didn't rotate around the Ryman Auditorium. Yet, where was I to find it?

Until I enrolled at Woodmont School, it had never occurred to me that I was a Yankee, the daughter of a celebrity, or anything else unusual. Nor had it occurred to me that I "talked funny."

But children, unfortunately, can be cruel. Not just children at Woodmont School, but children everywhere. At the edge of adolescence, they're often unthinking and clannish and quick to attack anything that's inconsistent with their usual world.

I remember now that, while we were living in Chicago, I'd visited my grandparents in Kentucky and thought to myself that people *there* "talked funny." Everyone, it seemed to me, should talk the way *I* did. And, if a Nashvillian had moved to Chicago, I'm sure I would have thought that that person "talked funny." I hadn't learned then that, even as beauty is in the eye of the beholder, talking "funny" is in the ear of the listener, and that what's the norm in one place is outlandish in another.

However, on my first day at Woodmont, I got the message. And since I was terribly insecure and didn't really like myself at all, the problem of making friends was even more difficult. It's almost impossible to sell something you can't endorse personally, and I had no confidence in myself.

Complicating my social life even further was my mother's illness. In addition to having a bad heart, Mom had a nervous breakdown; and, unless you've lived with a thing like that, you can't imagine what it's like.

An adolescent is basically selfish; so, at twelve (and later) I was more concerned about whether my mother understood me than I was about whether I understood *her*. As a matter of fact, during our first years in Nashville, the more people advised me I had to "understand" Mom, the greater the barrier became between us.

Other girls my age could have friends come to their houses to spend the night and could have parties and club meetings in their homes, but I never could. I could seldom even spend the night with other girls, and I adjusted to this restriction so completely that it still affects me.

When our daughters want friends to spend the night at our house or they want to spend the night away from home, I can't quite understand it. Sometimes I've asked them, "But at night you'll be asleep and won't be seeing your friend, so why do you and she want to spend the night together?"

Pat understands how the girls feel because he and his friends were constantly spending the night with each other, and he says that's part of the fun of growing up. But he grew up in a home without any serious problems. As a boy, he never met death or serious illness or any tragedy. The Boones lived in a little, white frame house where they had company all the time and more food than they could eat. Pat's mother had the stove just loaded with food, and the whole family was so hospitable that a visitor began to eat the minute he walked in the door!

It seemed to me at my house, by contrast, we had to be quiet and very careful of what we did and said lest we disturb Mom. The specter of death lurked in the silent shadows. So my teen years and Pat's were totally different, just as my adolescent years were different from those of the children I knew at Woodmont.

Among them I tried to win friends in two ways, one of which was a big mistake. My first move was to try to lose my Northern accent. Slowly, I stretched my vowels and dropped my *g*'s. Still I couldn't lose the tag *Yankee*. I was a stranger in a strange land, unaccustomed to the local folkways and, I'm afraid, a little bit self-righteous about it.

One day, for example, I got up to give my seat on a bus to an elderly Negro woman who'd gotten on. I'd been taught to respect my elders without reference to race, and I was startled and angry when I realized that the woman *couldn't* take my seat because it was in the "white section" of the bus.

The fact that Negroes lived in poor, run-down sections of Nashville offended me, and in this respect I may have been unduly smug, for they also lived in the slums of Chicago which were just as bad, perhaps worse, than the poorer sections of any Southern city, and that hadn't bothered me a bit. Actually, I hadn't even thought about it.

Probably my awareness of the condition of Negroes in Nashville was simply a part of my developing social consciousness, a part of my growing up. And, if I'd continued to live in Chicago, I guess I would have been just as disturbed by circumstances there. However, as things worked out, my criticism was directed at Nashville rather than at Chicago, and it didn't add to my popularity in my new hometown.

My second maneuver in my "love Shirley" campaign was to brag about being Red Foley's daughter. And that effort backfired horribly. In a family-conscious town, it seemed to me, my connection with an important Grand Ole·Opry star should open every door. So, casually (and not so casually), I let classmates know who my dad was.

Not surprisingly, the other kids couldn't care less, and they backed off.

As far as family connections went, I'd missed an important point. The children with the most prestigious family backgrounds were so sure of what they had that they rarely talked about it, just as people from long time wealthy families seldom are the big spenders because they don't have to impress anybody.

But here I was, a lonely, self-disparaging little girl who wanted so desperately to impress somebody. I tried so hard that I became lonelier than ever.

One occasion comes back to me as a particular nightmare—the night of the Junior Miss Club's dance. The affair wasn't especially sophisticated. The girls invited the boys, and parents carted the couples to and from the party. At that stage, I had absolutely no "clothes sense," and my mother had been sick too long to pay much attention to what I was wearing. During my earliest years, Mom had played with me like a doll, taking enormous pains to curl my hair and dress me nicely. However, by the time we moved to Nashville, her illness had depleted her energy until she was scarcely aware of what other girls in our neighborhood were wearing. Besides, she had a streak of German thrift and saw no reason to buy something new for me to wear to the Junior Miss Club dance. For that matter, neither did I.

My Aunt Connie had just sent a box of hand-me-downs, and my mother selected a dress which was new to me and one which she considered completely appropriate for the dance. It was tomato-red with a huge white collar, and I thought it looked very nice—at least around home.

I *did* secretly suspect that some of the girls in the club were going to shave their legs for the dance and wear hose.

But, because I was embarrassed to ask my mother if I could borrow her razor, I submissively put on my black Mary Jane slippers with, I think, white ankle socks. It would have been exciting to have shaved my legs, I thought, but still, surrounded only by my family, I considered Aunt Connie's dress OK.

When I got to the dance, though, I realized my mistake!

My date, a blond, blue-eyed Jewish boy whose father was a hair-stylist, was very sweet about it, but from the minute we walked through the door and *saw the other girls*, it was obvious that my clothes were terrible.

When you're twelve, you don't look to the future. The instant—the right now—is what counts, and every mistake is unendurable, serious far beyond its real merit. So when I saw the other girls with their shaved legs and nylon hose and absolutely-perfect-for-the-occasion dresses, I wanted to become invisible.

Yes, I'd heard all the slogans: "Pretty is as pretty does," "Beauty is only skin deep" and "Don't be fooled by appearances." But at that moment I felt that my appearance and my true self exactly matched. Each was a mess that should have stayed at home.

I know now that the horrible feeling of being a misfit is something almost every youngster—even the most popular and self-assured—experiences at some time or other, and I only wish there were some way every adolescent could understand this before he or she has to suffer the ordeal.

A friend, also from Nashville, remembers the first dance she ever attended. It was given by her best friend, who'd never been to a dance before either. As far as my friend was concerned, it was a disaster because when she got there, she discovered that: (1) She was the only girl present who'd been delivered to the door by her father *without* an escort! (2) She was the only girl wearing a short dress. (3) She was the only girl wearing low-heeled, black patent-leather slippers *and socks!*

These discoveries were dreadful enough, but conditions got worse. Since she had no escort, my friend settled in a corner to watch in mortification as the couples danced past her while she wondered how long it would be before her father would come to take her home.

She had an enormous crush on her hostess' older brother who'd never paid any attention to her except when they occasionally played on the same touch-football team. However, as she sat miserably in her corner, this handsome creature (at least fourteen years old) whirled by with a sensitive and kindly disposed girl.

"Billy," said the good Samaritan girl, pointing at the unhappy child in the corner, "why don't you dance with her?"

"Naw," her partner retorted, "she doesn't want to dance."

"Yes she does."

"No she doesn't."

Meanwhile, the couple had come to a halt and were studying the unfortunate misfit as though she were a laboratory specimen. Under their analytical stares, her ankle socks seemed to be growing until she was sure that pretty soon other people would be tripping on them.

"You don't want to dance, do you?" the apple of her eye demanded in the tone he'd once used when she'd failed to halt a line drive over center. (Being chubby, she sometimes played center.)

"No."

It took her months to realize that her first dance hadn't ruined her life. And it was years before she found courage to dance with her best friend's brother.

Mia Farrow told in an interview about the agony of her first important outing with her peers. The Farrow family had just returned from Spain and England after several years abroad when Mia was invited to a Beverly Hills—Bel-Air dance. Mia's mother, Maureen O'Sullivan Farrow, took great pains with her daughter's clothes for the occasion and, since she herself had been the belle of the movie set when she'd come to California as a girl, she assumed that Mia would have as much fun with the Hollywood crowd as she'd always had.

Mia, encouraged by her mother, dutifully went to the dance and valiantly tried to be friendly, but, she has recalled, "My clothes were wrong; my conversation was wrong. Nothing about me was right."

Finally, after every other girl had been invited to dance, but she'd been left against the wall, Mia crept home and hid in the garage until she thought the party would be over. Then, with imitation gaiety, she walked into the house and, to her mother's question, "Did you have a good time?" gave a convincing, "Yes." At that moment she proved herself as an actress.

In one way, the experiences of these other girls aren't a part of my story, and yet they are because they're a part of the story of practically every girl in the world. Almost every adolescent is insecure and lonely at times and thinks that her life is ruined.

When I was thirteen, I was introduced to Pat Boone for the first time. But three years later when we met again, he didn't remember that he'd ever seen me before—which gives you an idea of what I was like.

I had just about decided that I was a hopeless mess, a girl who'd never be popular, when at the end of my first year at Woodmont *I unexpectedly became a heroine.* One night while I was baby-sitting with a doctor's children, a man broke into the house, and I was instrumental in his arrest. Because it was quite late, the baby of the family was sleeping in his crib and I had slipped upstairs and crawled into bed with his two sisters.

I heard someone downstairs, and I was terrified because I knew the doctor and his wife hadn't come home. If they had come in, they'd be talking and they would have come straight upstairs to see about the children. But the person below (I was sure it was only one person) was moving stealthily—like a burglar!

I heard the prowler climbing the steps, and fear almost nauseated me. Instinctively, I began to pray. For, out of the unhappiness and trouble I'd experienced, I'd clung to a constantly increasing faith in God.

When the burglar came into the room where I lay with the sleeping children, I was praying hard, and God certainly heard and answered me. Because, acting through instinct, not reason, I followed the safest and sanest course. Through the greatest conscious effort, I kept my eyes shut, my body relaxed and my breathing even, so that when the burglar glanced at me, he thought I was asleep.

He lit a match and rummaged through dresser drawers while I continued my silent prayer. Then assuming I'd slept through his search, he went back downstairs.

I've often wondered what would have happened if one of the little sisters had awakened or if the baby had begun to cry while that man was in the house, because, as I later learned, he was drunk and armed with a gun. Or, what would have happened to the children and me if I'd really been asleep when he'd entered the house and awakened with a start when he'd struck that match?

As soon as I was sure the intruder had gone back downstairs, I took a dangerous chance to reach the phone, which was in another second-floor bedroom.

Two factors impelled me. I felt a responsibility to the doctor for the safety of his household while I was in charge, so I didn't want anything stolen. But, more than that, I was afraid the man would come upstairs again and discover that I wasn't really sleeping.

Silently I slipped out of bed and, crawling along on my stomach, inched past the stairwell to the room with the telephone. Then, holding a pillow around the phone so that the burglar wouldn't hear, I called the police.

The intruder left the house before the police arrived, but they caught him still in the neighborhood with items he'd stolen from the doctor, so they knew they had the right man.

The next day the newspapers carried the story on the front page: "Teenage Baby-Sitter Saves Three Children." Out of a clear blue sky, I was a celebrity. People began to speak to me who'd never spoken before. And, reading the flattering news accounts of my adventure, I even began to think better of myself.

Nevertheless, I didn't immediately find the friends and sense of security I wanted so badly. I had to wait for those until I entered West High School and met a wonderful man named Coach Strickland.

4
Two Steps Forward, One Step Back

"And now," the beaming principal said, "I'd like to introduce our guest for today. He's not only a famous man whose talent we've all enjoyed on radio and records, but he's the father of one of our own students. So let's give a big welcome to Grand Ole Opry star, Red Foley—father of West High's own Shirley Foley."

The West High students were gathered for assembly, and as the principal, Dr. Yarborough, introduced my father, a dark nagging fear crept over me. I was proud of my dad and I loved him, but as my classmates half turned to smile at me while they applauded my dad, months rolled back and, in imagination, I was once again at Woodmont. There I'd been a lonely Yankee and, as I'd unwisely boasted too often, "Red Foley's daughter."

But at West High my world had been different, thanks primarily to one fine man—Coach Emmett Strickland. At West, unlike Woodmont, I'd lost much of my self-consciousness. I'd been happy. Why, I'd even been popular!

And all without telling one soul that my father was famous.

Before leaving Woodmont, I'd realized that my efforts to win friends had been misguided and that nobody was going to like me just because I was Red Foley's daughter. So when I enrolled at West, I resolved to keep my family connections a secret, as much as possible. I didn't lie about my parentage and, as a matter of fact, I imagine most students realized that my dad was a Country Western entertainer.

However, before any of my classmates had found time to decide what they thought of me, I met Coach Strickland, who, through his encouragement, had helped me discover a personality of my own. I don't know yet how he became aware of my terrible insecurity and my need for reassurance. With so many students to think about, it's amazing that he should have sensed my fright and hunger for approval. But, one day early in my first term, he stopped me in the hall and said, "Shirley, we're having tryouts for cheerleaders this afternoon, and I want you to be there."

Me? A cheerleader?

For a wild moment, I thought he must have mistaken me for someone else, but his kind smile told me that he hadn't.

"I—I can't—" I almost whispered. I was so awed by the honor of the mere suggestion that I might become one of the peppy, popular girls who drew cheers and applause from the rest of the student body that I was almost voiceless.

"Of course you can," Coach Strickland insisted. "I think you may be just what the cheering section needs. So—and this is an order—you be at tryouts this afternoon."

Madly longing to be a cheerleader but terrified of the rejection I knew was sure to come, I reported to the tryouts. Coach Strickland was there, of course, and, when he saw me, he smiled so warmly I knew I couldn't leave. In fact, I suddenly felt almost competitive. I wanted to do well—be the best, even—in return for the coach's confidence. If such a wise and wonderful man thought I had potential, well, I'd have to muster whatever assets I had rather than disappoint him. I gave it everything I had.

When the afternoon ended, I almost danced toward home! For, wonder of wonders, I—*I, Shirley Foley,* the Yankee outcast, had been chosen as a cheerleader! The fact that other students had liked me, had thought I was good, gave me more self-confidence than I'd known since we'd moved to Nashville. Only the last-minute recollection that my mother might not be feeling well kept me from shouting and banging the door behind me as I rushed into our house.

For almost everyone, I suspect, the remembrance of high school years presents a panorama of sunny, soaring peaks and dark, devastating valleys—moments of almost uncontrollable, joyous excitement balanced by times of stabbing pain. And, for me, the day I redeemed Coach Strickland's faith in me by being chosen cheerleader is a radiant mountaintop in my memory.

I didn't have a crush on the coach the way some girls do on high school faculty members, but I loved him dearly because he taught me to feel more kindly toward myself. Somehow he drew me out of my shell so that I could develop into a person. Largely as a result of his encouragement, I was chosen cheerleader every year I was at West and was also elected as one of West's "superlatives," which meant I was (technically at least) one of the most popular girls in school.

Every small triumph gave me more confidence in myself, so that, after just one year of high school, I'd practically forgotten the loneliness I'd experienced at Woodmont. I felt socially safe until that shattering day when I was introduced during assembly as Red Foley's daughter! As I write now that the principal's introduction upset me, it sounds horribly silly. But still, as the other students craned their necks in my direction, I felt like Cinderella when she heard the clock strike midnight.

Everything's ruined! I thought in ridiculous panic. I

managed a stiff smile. *Now nobody will accept me for myself anymore.* Happily, neither my father nor Dr. Yarborough realized what I was thinking, nor did the other students. They continued to treat me exactly the way they'd treated me before and, in the days that followed, I discovered with relief that my father's fame couldn't hurt me at West—anymore than it had *helped* me at Woodmont.

It's a little frightening, perhaps, to discover that you are going to be judged for yourself alone and not because of some extra trappings, but it's also heartening, because, under those circumstances when you get into trouble, you know exactly whom to blame: Yourself.

My years at West High School were happy ones, but not perfectly so. For one thing, my mother's illness grew more critical. I felt increasing responsibility for my little sisters and, predictably, I made mistakes!

I was a girl who resented discipline, and the results hurt *me* more than they hurt anyone else. Looking back, I think my resentment stemmed from at least three things: First, I was an adolescent, at an age when young people traditionally resent authority.

Next, the authority I was under at home was rather hit-and-miss since my father traveled a great deal and my mother was sick so much of the time that she couldn't apply evenhanded, consistent discipline. As a matter of fact, forced so often by circumstances to take charge of my sisters, I often felt like self-appointed head of the household.

Then, finally, though I went to church and prayed regularly, I hadn't at that time learned that discipline is a gift from God. God has established orders of authority (a wife should be submissive to her husband; children to their parents and teachers) for our own happiness. In addition, as Chaplain Merlin R. Carothers points out in his book, *Prison to Praise,* restraints and burdens which we tend to find galling are actually blessings if only we will look at them that way. Col. Carothers urges in his book that we praise

42

God for seeming burdens as well as for apparent blessings, for, in God's plan, all things work for our good.[1]

As a teenager, though, I never thought of restraints and burdens as blessings. So instead of praising God for the authority I encountered, I fumed and sometimes rebelled.

There was the matter of a teacher who, I thought, had treated me unfairly. Who knows? Maybe she had; on the other hand, she may have been perfectly fair, while I, from my biased vantage point, couldn't see it. In any case, I brooded over the way I imagined I was being mistreated until I literally felt sick every time I saw the teacher in question. If, for some unavoidable reason, I had to speak with her, knots formed in my stomach.

This went on for a while until at last, unable to tolerate the discomfort caused purely by my own rebellion, I went contritely to the teacher and asked to talk with her about our misunderstanding.

Within a few minutes we were friends again, and for days afterward I reveled in my freedom from anger. I won't deny that you can get a certain dark satisfaction from holding a grudge, but it can't compare with the satisfaction that comes from *forgetting* one.

This experience has already helped me in counseling my girls when they've had personality conflicts with some of their teachers. I've told them to accept it as part of their education—a challenge—an opportunity to learn how to win their teachers' respect and friendship. God's class in human relations!

When I was about fourteen or fifteen, my rebellion against discipline reached a climax. Like Cherry, I ran away from home. But, very unlike her, I didn't do it in a spirit of love, nor in quest of God. If I'd been hunting for the devil, I would have found him right away because he was with me, prompting me. However, I wasn't looking for anything except freedom from authority.

The mountain I finally created began with a molehill. I'd spilled ink; my mother had scolded me, and I'd talked back to her. At that age, I guess I thought I was too good to be fussed at, because wasn't that what my honors at school signified? So it seemed to me. Anyway, I did the one thing my father absolutely forbade above all else—I talked back to my mother. The Foley temper and the Shirley mouth had done it again!

I guess the thing Daddy spanked me for most often was for talking back. Therefore, after I'd spilled the ink and been ordered to my room for "sassing," I was scared.

Mom had threatened, "I'll let your daddy take care of you," and I knew he *would*—good and proper. I knew, too, that I'd been wrong, and that increased my fright.

Therefore, acting more instinctively than rationally, and seething yet with rebellion, I lifted a screen from the window, climbed out and ran away. I was feeling very, very sorry for myself as I hurried off with no firm goal in mind.

Since I had to go somewhere, I headed for the home of my best girl friend which, luckily, was a long walk away. I say "luckily" because the walk gave me time to think about the seriousness of what I was doing. I'd scarcely gone a dozen steps from home before I wanted to turn around and go back, but I was afraid to. I'd already taken such a drastic step, that now I had to follow through.

My walk took me across a golf course, and as I marched along, scarcely conscious of whether I was on a green or a fairway, I grew more and more frightened at what I'd done. What, I wondered, would Daddy do now? Suppose, by my unthinking conduct, I'd caused Mom to have a relapse and maybe even die. Could my parents ever forgive me, or would they punish me for running away for the rest of my life?

Plagued by such thoughts, I was certain that I could never go home again. Never! I would ask my girl friend to hide me, I decided. The idea was ridiculous, but I planned to make her promise not to tell anyone where I was.

Tears rolled down my cheeks as, in my fancies, I became a tragic heroine—the Poor Little Match Girl huddling alone on a corner, Little Orphan Annie, keeping her identity a secret from her loved ones as she watched them from a distance. Luxuriating in self-pity, I imagined my parents peeping sadly into my empty room, and I grew genuinely homesick as I thought of my very own bed, the one I might never sleep in again.

Well, not for weeks anyway.

My girl friend, not knowing what else to do with me, took me to the home of her brother or sister. I'm not sure now which it was, nor can I remember exactly why we went there. Maybe her parents weren't at home.

Since I'd never before visited the family to which we turned, I was certain my parents couldn't find me at their house. However, they didn't have to find me because some adult in the group had already called Daddy and told him where I was. Then, to my combined relief and despair, someone took me home. I'd run away by broad daylight, but it was dark when I got back.

I'd already talked with Daddy by phone, and he'd been understanding.

"Honey," he'd said, "you just come on home, and we'll talk things over."

"Promise you won't spank me," I'd begged.

He'd agreed.

"Your mom has been so worried, she's very, very sick," he'd told me. "She's in bed now. Hurry up, honey, just come on home."

It must have taken all his willpower to keep from blistering me when I finally walked through the door, but he kept his promise. However, to punish me, he made me give up some of my school activities for a while. For a prescribed period, I had to forego being a cheerleader and a ROTC sponsor—and that hurt worse than a spanking!

Aside from troubles I brought on myself, I only suffered two big disappointments while I was going to West. The first involved a sorority. Happily, and with considerable pride, I joined one, but later I was so disappointed when my sorority sisters refused membership to one of my friends that I resigned. My friend, incidentally, eventually *was* initiated into that very sorority, and in time became its president.

My other and biggest disappointment came in my junior year when my father told me I'd have to change schools at midterm. My mother was about to undergo open-heart surgery and, during the time of her most critical illness, Daddy thought my sisters and I would be better off in boarding school than living at home.

I was crushed! My friends, my social life, my honors—everything was at West. And, to top it all, so was my favorite boyfriend, a high school basketball star named Don Johnson. If I left West, I was sure my life would be ruined.

Nevertheless, because I had to, I transferred to David Lipscomb as a boarding student, and the first night I was there I had a date with Pat Boone.

Romans 8:28!

5
One Puff Too Many

God's plan for all creation is perfect.

Whether you consider the perfect balance of the stars, the perfect way in which nature renews itself as the seasons pass, or the operation of cause and effect in the life of an individual, God's hand and wisdom are strikingly evident.

In your own life, you've probably made decisions through impulse which produced results more exciting than you could ever have foreseen or imagined—thanks to a loving mind much greater than your own.

I realize now that the Holy Spirit, constantly at work in the world, protects and directs those who permit Him. However, when I was sixteen and a casual puff of smoke reversed my direction, the Holy Spirit never entered my mind. Nevertheless, if some girl whose identity I'll never know hadn't smoked one cigarette too many, I probably wouldn't be where I am today—Pat Boone's wife and the mother of his daughters.

In fact, except for a casual billow of smoke, Pat and I

might never even have dated. I doubt that our girls have considered how much they owe to a bygone smoker who may have long since given up cigarettes. But, believe me, they owe her a lot.

During the summer when I was thirteen years old and about to enter the ninth grade, Mom was sicker than usual, so sick that she and Dad decided she would return to a hospital in Chicago for a few weeks while I'd be placed in a boarding school.

Since I was so young, my parents looked for a school which would give me careful supervision. And they certainly found one—David Lipscomb, operated by Church of Christ people.

The faculty was kind but strict. I was homesick and worried about my mother, so my summer at Lipscomb was a miserable one. As the school's youngest boarding student that term, I was so closely supervised that I could only leave the campus to go to the drugstore, *and that with a chaperone.*

During the unhappy summer, however, something nice did happen. A friend named Julia Bradshaw introduced me to a friend of hers, a thirteen-year-old boy named Pat Boone who was a Lipscomb student during the regular school term. He was wearing a baseball uniform because he'd been playing baseball in Centennial Park, and I was enormously impressed. So good-looking and an athlete besides!

However, not even meeting a cute boy who might be in my classes in the fall was enough to make me like Lipscomb and want to stay there a minute longer than necessary. So, when fall came, I was delighted to go home to my family and enroll in West High School where I was to spend two and a half wonderful years.

I was a junior at West when Mom's condition became so critical that doctors recommended open-heart surgery, a brand-new medical procedure.

Poor Dad. Now as I look back at his ordeal, I can understand what he went through much better than I could at the time. A weaker man might have broken down entirely under the burdens he was forced to carry, but somehow—though he was distraught about Mom—he managed after a fashion to look after my sisters and me, mostly by letting us know that he loved us.

When he told us that we'd have to transfer to boarding schools until Mom was better, though I was heartbroken, we knew that he was acting in the best interest of the family. We knew it, but the knowledge didn't relieve the hurt as far as I was concerned. For I not only had friends and honors at West, I had my beau, Don Johnson.

Since my sisters were still in grade school, there was no question as to where they'd enroll: St. Cecelia's, a Catholic school which provided boarding care for grammar school students. I, though, was given a choice of three schools: David Lipscomb, Ward-Belmont and Peabody.

For some reason I can't remember, I never considered Peabody at all, nor did I consider David Lipscomb. Not at first. My summer there had been such an unhappy one for me that I thought I never wanted to see the place again.

My initial vote went to Ward-Belmont because it was the alma mater of Grand Ole Opry star Minnie Pearl, a friend of our family. Ward-Belmont was the offspring of two very fine old schools for girls, Belmont College and Ward's Seminary, and for generations it had been a strict institution dedicated to the education and refinement of young ladies. In prior years, Ward-Belmont girls had been required to wear either black or dark blue whenever they'd left the campus (conservative, decent apparel suitable for a lady appearing in public), and they had been chaperoned even at church. Further, they wore gloves but no makeup.

Believe it or not, both Minnie Pearl and Grace Moore of the movies had been students there under such conventlike conditions and loved it! However, at the time I might have enrolled, Ward-Belmont was in a transitional stage which had produced a greatly relaxed atmosphere.

Dr. Yarborough, the principal at West, was a member of the Church of Christ and was urging me to go to Lipscomb. Yet, as much as I loved him, I couldn't forget how much I'd disliked the place, so I told him, "No, I think I'll go to Ward-Belmont."

Dad, despite the hours he had to spend working and with Mom and her doctors, went with me to inspect the school I'd tentatively chosen. Our visit began pleasantly enough. Everyone on the attractive campus was cordial. But as our tour progressed, my enthusiasm dwindled. Minnie Pearl or no Minnie Pearl, Ward-Belmont made me uncomfortable.

Its alumnae from the era when students got demerits for not sitting up straight in chapel will find this hard to believe, but the way many of the girls were dressed that day raised our eyebrows (too tight sweaters and skirts), the language of some of the students seemed shockingly coarse, and the campus "smoker" seemed such a distasteful climax to our visit that I was convinced I was in the wrong place.

It's impossible to explain my reaction to the lounge which our guide identified as "the Smoker" except to say that it was part of God's plan. To tell the truth, the sight of girls smoking had never bothered me before. In fact, some of my friends at West smoked. Yet, in the lounge at Ward-Belmont, just one girl too many was enjoying just one puff more than I could tolerate. Not one particular girl, not a particular puff that I can recall triggered my reaction, but suddenly *I knew that Ward-Belmont just wasn't for me.*

I don't tell this story to flaunt my own virtue, because my virtue had nothing to do with it; and, actually, the incident when set down coldly on paper makes me sound like a prissy, holier-than-thou snob. I've included the story because it illustrates the workings of the Holy Spirit. I'm certain, looking back, that if smoking hadn't forced my decision in favor of Lipscomb, something else would have, for God was gently turning me in that direction.

When Daddy said, "You can go wherever you want," I was almost surprised to hear myself answering, "I want to go back to David Lipscomb."

Yes, I still remembered how the restrictions there had galled me, but I also remembered a spirit of love which had pervaded the school. I believed that I was sophisticated and able to handle my life without rules and regulations, that I didn't need the atmosphere of a church-oriented school. Yet God knew better, so with "friendly persuasion" He directed me to Lipscomb.

I chose Lipscomb over Ward-Belmont and Peabody. Nevertheless, I transferred from West with reluctance. In fact, knowing that I wouldn't be able to see Don every day seemed awful.

Someday, if one of my daughters suffering the loss of a teenage love should say, "But, Mother, you don't know what its like!"—how wrong she'll be.

Yet the misery I felt upon being separated from Don was nothing compared to the misery I'd know in the months ahead. The misery, the excitement and the joy! For at Lipscomb I was to discover emotion and depths of emotion far beyond any I'd imagined. I couldn't foresee the outcome, but the cornerstone for all that emotion was set within hours of my return to the school when my roommate, Betsy Moss, reintroduced me to Pat Boone.

Betsy and I were standing in the hall when Pat walked up and asked to meet me, totally unaware that we'd met before. I remembered, but I was so willing to overlook the lapse that, when he asked me to go sledding with him that night, I said I'd be delighted.

Here again God took a hand in things because Nashville, which doesn't get snow often, had just gotten such a heavy fall that school was being let out because of the unusual weather. So a group of boys and girls were going sledding, using Pat's house as a base, since his parents welcomed crowds and always had plenty of homemade goodies on hand.

If Nashville hadn't gotten snow just then—it—well, if practically *any* detail had been different, my future and Pat's too might have been quite different. Perhaps we would have fallen in love and gotten married regardless of the weather. But sledding is such fun and a sledding date so informal that our relationship got off to the best possible start.

I didn't forget Don immediately, but as I flew down a hill on a sled with Pat, Don was harder to remember. And the difficulty increased every day.

Though Don was a star athlete and a nice boy, so was Pat; in addition, Pat could sing! More than that, Pat was cartoonist for the school paper, a frequent soloist with the school chorus, a top student, a campus leader and a good-looking guy. In short, he was just about everything any girl could want, so I was tremendously pleased by his immediate interest in me.

Since the Lipscomb campus was small and Pat and I both sang with the chorus, we were thrown together often. Right off the bat we began dating regularly, and by the time school was out, we knew that we cared very deeply for each other. At least I was sure that I cared deeply for *him*, and I thought and prayed that he felt the same way about me. But with Pat you couldn't be certain.

In the first place, he wasn't a fast kind of guy a girl had to battle every time she got into his car. In fact, if Pat so much as held a girl's hand in public everybody knew she was "special!" I like the fact that he didn't automatically turn a date into a wrestling match, but, on the other hand, because he wasn't as demonstrative as some fellows, I couldn't take his affection for granted. Further, I wasn't the only girl he dated, and that kept me on my toes.

I dated other boys, but that wasn't so much through choice. Rather, it was because of Pat's aggravating habit of asking for dates at the last minute. More than once I'd be *sure* that he was going to ask me for a date for a special event or for a particular night, and I'd eagerly wait for him to speak up. But, finally, as the night in question approached and he hadn't said a word, I'd agree to go out with somebody else, only to have Pat, at long last, make his move. Too late!

Having to tell him I was busy was torture, especially since I knew he'd find another date with no trouble. But because he'd been slow in speaking, I'd have to say no to what I wanted more than almost anything—precious hours with the boy I was learning to love.

Pat procrastinated because he was playing it safe. He didn't want to take a chance on being turned down, so he'd ask everybody, including my roommate, whether I had a date—before he asked me. However, his delaying tactics had exactly the opposite effect of what he'd intended. They almost guaranteed that I'd *have* a date by the time he got around to asking for one!

I'll never forget what he put me through just before our big junior-senior banquet. I was absolutely certain that Pat was going to ask me to go with him. But he hadn't when, a month before the banquet, another boy asked, "Shirley, do you have a date for the banquet?"

Because he asked it so bluntly, I had to tell him that I didn't and that he could be my escort. That time Pat's delay hurt me deeply.

As a matter of fact, almost every time something really important was coming up, Pat would put off asking for a date until it was too late. He didn't seem to realize that, where a big event was concerned, *other* boys asked for dates *early*.

In addition to holding so many other honors, Pat was a letterman and president of the "M" Club ("M for Lipscomb Mustangs), so I really looked forward to being his date for the club's hayride. You know how much fun a hayride can be, especially with the right "one." However, as usual, when Pat finally asked me to go with him, I already had a date.

That was bad enough; but, to make matters harder to bear, Pat then asked my girl friend, the one he'd been dating when we first met at the age of thirteen! I knew they'd been very close then, so the idea of them going on a hayride together was hard to swallow. But, the worst was yet to come!

The hayride was to be on somebody's farm near Murfreesboro and, when we began climbing onto the truck for the trip, we discovered there wasn't room for everyone; so Pat and his date volunteered to go in his car! Torture again.

That night was a nightmare for me.

It would have been agonizing to have watched Pat with another girl on the truck, but to know that he was with another girl in his car where I couldn't watch them was practically unbearable.

The boy I was with had a great personality, so I tried to make the best of a bad situation. However, I can promise you, ours wasn't a typical hayride date. We spent the evening yodeling.

The night of the hayride, the night of the junior-senior banquet—I remember each as painful. But they didn't bring the tears I was to shed later.

My mother's death when I was seventeen and the romantic problems Pat and I faced almost immediately afterward made my senior year in high school a period of testing and heartbreak.

And it was also a time for growing up—fast.

6

Hello, Mom—Goodbye

I wish I had understood my mother better.

Just before she died we had a talk—almost our last—which gave me a glimpse of what an understanding might have meant, not only during the awkward, adolescent years when I'd been insecure and friendless, but in the coming months when I, a girl wildly in love with Pat and longing to marry him, would consider it my duty to give him up.

When summer came after my first regular term at Lipscomb, Pat went to visit his grandparents in Jacksonville, Florida, and I missed him like crazy, especially since he wrote sweet, adorable letters to me filled with his silly sense of humor which I love. Since he's a first-rate cartoonist, he sometimes made sketches on the envelopes, crazy things which made me laugh even while I wanted so badly to see him that I was ready to cry. Once he wrote that he was being sculpted and would send me the result. He sent a coconut with a monkey face carved on it.

When he came back to Nashville we resumed our dating, and for a while there were only two real obstacles to my happiness. The first was my mother's poor health, which really hadn't been improved by surgery. The other was my resistance to the Church of Christ. I loved Pat, and he and other friends at school assured me that their church was the only path to heaven. But that doctrine was one of the very things I held against it. No matter how open I was to persuasion, I simply wasn't convinced that everyone outside its membership was going to hell. My mother? My daddy? My sisters and so many other God-fearing people I loved, *going to hell?* Impossible!

For the best possible reason, the kids at school worked hard to bring me from my Baptist background into the Church of Christ. Love was their first motive. They believed they had the key to salvation, and they wanted to share it with me. However, I felt that I'd gotten to know the Lord pretty well before I'd come to Lipscomb, so I sometimes felt offended when my friends insisted that only members of "their church" would go to heaven. I was convinced then—as I am now—that *nobody's own efforts and understanding* will get him or her into heaven, and that anyone who believes this is in trouble! For *only God's grace and Jesus' blood* will open up the gate.

Actually, while I was at Lipscomb I had a rather easygoing disposition. I generally believed the best about everybody, so I concluded that if my friends felt they absolutely had to convert me to the Church of Christ, OK. After all, they were acting through love. Still, I asked questions and, when I didn't get satisfactory answers, I remembered. Those unanswered questions ate at me and made me uneasy toward Pat's beloved church.

Their view of Billy Graham was one of the attitudes which really shattered me. How *could* these people, I wondered, judge a man like Billy and say he was lost because he hadn't done this or that? Whether Billy Graham or anyone else was lost, I thought, was between that person and God; so the harsh and final judgment I heard expressed really wounded me.

I knew that my mother, who'd grown up in the Salvation Army, had a deep, real relationship with God. Her faith was an intrinsic part of her. And my daddy had been brought up as a Baptist and loved God too.

In trying to accept the Church of Christ doctrine, I sometimes wondered whether I were doing it just to please Pat. I sincerely hoped that I'd never use religion that way, but maybe I did, for even the apostle Paul said that he didn't know his own heart. Since I'm not sure to this day that I know *my* heart, I can only pray a lot for God's mercy.

Anyway, I tried to accept the teachings I got at Lipscomb with a loving spirit; still, I questioned. I remembered how the disciples had come to Jesus one day, saying, "Master, there's one casting out demons in your name, and he's not one of *us.*" (Mark 9:38-40).

Then Jesus had said, "He who is not against us is for us. '

And, remembering that, I thought, *Well, now, doesn't that apply to Billy Graham?* That was one of the questions eating at me.

When I remembered what love and compassion Jesus had felt for people and how He'd said that if you give a man a drink of water or do this or that for him, "You are doing it for me," I couldn't help feeling that Billy Graham was giving the kind of help Jesus had in mind. Yet, so many of my friends were writing him off as lost, as a "false prophet."

I couldn't do that. I could never sit in judgment on another man. While I strongly believe that the Word of God is the truth which we must obey according to our understanding, I also believe in a loving, merciful and just God. I've always felt that way, so I couldn't believe that it was up to *me* to decide who was going to make it into heaven and who wasn't.

The efforts of my friends at Lipscomb to save me from

hell sometimes got to be more than I could take. One night, for instance, after I'd gone bowling with a boy, he asked me at my door whether I'd go to church with him the next morning.

My answer must have shocked him because he hadn't sat in on all the dorm conversations and heard the barrage of doctrine I'd been getting.

"No, I won't go with you," I told him. "Now tell me I'm going to hell!"

Answering that way was against my nature, but at the moment I'd had as much as I could stand of warnings that I and my family were lost.

Finally, I think, I *went* to church with the boy I'd berated, as a sort of apology for my arrogance. Further, I truly wanted to believe what the Church of Christ taught because Pat said it was true and I'd already begun subconsciously to make Pat my god. That great sin produced disastrous results, though, years later.

As I mentioned earlier, Pat was very discriminating (or cautious) in his courtship, never one to force a lot of physical attention on a girl. If he showed affection, you knew he felt it. So he didn't even kiss me until we'd been dating regularly for about nine months! As a result, that kiss was terribly exciting because by that time it really meant something to both of us. It wasn't an average, normal date-type kiss; but, for that matter, nothing about our relationship was average or normal.

Since I had a good thing going, I didn't want to say anything to upset the situation; but I wondered when he was going to kiss me again. I didn't find out until three weeks later!

Yes, Pat *was* a cautious and discriminating suitor.

He and I played the leads in the senior play, "Annie Laurie," which sort of topped everything else that had happened. Though I'd been at Lipscomb a relatively short time, I'd been chosen a cheerleader and secretary of the student body; and starring in the senior play with a fellow like Pat was the cherry on the sundae. Especially since that fellow was *my* fellow.

Even Mom and Dad came to the play, making the occasion truly special for me, and afterward Pat and I were to attend a party at the home of a student, Bill Phillips, who lived a distance from town. At that time I was living at home under rules which included a curfew, and by the time we got to the party it was almost my curfew hour. However, since Pat and I had been leads in the play, and since another couple had ridden to the party with us in Pat's car, I was sure I could stay out later than usual. So I called home for permission.

I knew Mom and Dad would say, "Fine." But, to my despair, they didn't. If Mom hadn't been sick, I don't think she would have told me to come home at once, but you don't always think rationally when you're ill.

I was hurt. I was depressed. I *was furious.* I was being robbed of my glory and being embarrassed before my friends by totally unreasonable parents. Or that's how it seemed to me.

Pat took me home where I stormed into the house, slammed the door behind me, and went to my room without speaking to a soul. I was too immature to realize that I was hurting myself as much as anyone—maybe more.

The next day I prowled around the house, still not speaking to anybody, including my mother. But, as the day wore on, God began to deal with me. Gradually I came to realize how miserable I was making myself and how childishly I was behaving. A question began to hit me: "Why are you doing this? If you're out for vengeance, *you* may be getting it, because you're surely hurting your mother, but you're hurting yourself even *more.* Aren't you?"

Yes, I was.

My mother was asleep when I first realized how cruel and foolish I'd been. However, she awakened after a while, and I tiptoed into her room, mustering all my courage to make a confession.

"Mom," I said, sitting down on her bed, "I want to talk to you. I know now how selfish and unkind I've been, and I owe you an apology."

Mom sat up and took me in her arms. I'm not sure whether she was crying or not, but she said, "No, Shirley. It's I who owe you an apology. I should have come to you!"

Loving, clinging, understanding—at last, understanding—we shared precious moments together, almost the last moments we'd ever share on this earth. If only I'd known.

Not long afterward Mom died, and for a while we thought Dad might too. I'd half expected her death almost every day I could remember, so I should have been prepared for it. Yet Mom's dying was a shock I wasn't sure our family would survive. Suddenly I felt additional responsibility for my sisters, and even responsibility for Daddy. In fact, on some days I felt that I was the parent and *he* was the child.

During the bleak hours and days immediately following our loss, I thought often of God, and just as often of Pat, for both gave me comfort. Mom's eternal destiny was beyond me now; all I could do was trust the just and merciful God I'd come to know. On the other hand, I wasn't so sure how her oldest daughter was going to fare on earth.

Then Pat's mother reached out to me.

"Shirley," she said, "if you ever need a mother, come to me."

Further, Pat at long last committed himself. One night, soon after Mom's funeral, we'd come home from a ride and were sitting in his car in front of the house. There were post lights by our driveway, and any time I sat in a car for so much as sixty seconds, Dad began turning them off and on as a signal for me to come in.

On this night Pat saw the lights blink and knew we'd only

have a moment together. For once—finally—he lost his reserve, though not completely. He didn't propose marriage or make a passionate declaration, but he did say, "Shirley, I think I love you."

That was all. In fact, he didn't even ask me to go steady, but when I went into the house I was living the lyrics of every popular song. *I didn't know what time it was. Life was just a bowl of cherries. I had my love to keep me warm,* and *Zing! went the strings of my heart.* Or that's how it seemed.

Pat was all I could think of—all I'd want to think of for years and years.

7
Two Become One

This chapter is a most difficult one to write because unless I can find exactly the right words to convey what I have felt and what I feel, it may be misunderstood and bring unhappiness to several people I dearly love, Pat included.

But the truth of the matter is that when my mom died and Mrs. Boone offered to become my substitute mother, she didn't offer to be my mother-*in-law*. Far from it!

Quite sensibly, Pat's parents would have objected to his marriage to *anyone* while he was still in school. They rightly felt that he should finish his education and mature some more before he assumed responsibility for a wife and, more than likely, a house full of children.

He was so bright and had such remarkable potential that his mother and father were appalled by the thought that he might fall in love, marry, and drop out of school in order to support a family. So, when they saw that he and I were spending more and more time together—practically all of our free time—they objected.

I'm sure that every parent who has said to a teenage child, "You're too young to go steady," or "You should go out with other people and cultivate more friends," or "It's foolish to put all your eggs in one basket," can understand their concern.

The Boones wouldn't have liked it if Pat at seventeen had become too seriously involved with *any* girl; but, beyond that, they had special objections to his involvement with me. In the first place, the Boone and Foley backgrounds were as different as day and night. Pat's father was in the construction business, his mother a former nurse and full-time housewife. So show business was totally outside their understanding and experience. Life in Outer Mongolia couldn't have seemed more foreign to them than life on the Country-Western circuit. They didn't condemn my background as wrong, but they were afraid that Pat and I had too little in common to live happily ever after.

Today I realize that, in taking this stand, Mama and Daddy Boone weren't just thinking of Pat and themselves. They were thinking of me, too, and of how I'd also be hurt by an early and ill-advised marriage. And I respect them for the strength and love they evidenced in taking their stand.

Among many parents now, it's fashionable to allow teenage children to make their own decisions and tragic mistakes. And, I must say, the permissive philosophy sometimes looks very attractive to a harried mother or father who has had to hold the line against youthful pleas and tantrums. It would be so easy to tell a child, "Do whatever you want to. You must decide."

However, the Boones were too loving and too conscientious to take such an easy way out.

So, instead of looking the other way and hoping the danger would go away, they warned Pat that a serious romance could ruin his future and urged him not to date me so much. They preached the importance of an education and reminded him that early marriage might rob him of his, while at the same time they reminded him of my heredity. Since my mother had been ill so many years, wasn't it possible that I'd inherited some organic weakness which would make me a sickly wife and the mother of sickly children? Pat, his parents urged, should think about that. As indeed he should have.

And, due to my mother's illness, she suffered through emotional breakdowns which affected my emotional stability. I'm sure Pat's folks were concerned about all of these circumstances that could take their toll on our future—should we decide to share it. And besides, we were so *young*!

Actually, the Boones weren't the *only* ones who thought Pat and I should see less of each other. My dad didn't approve of steady dating either; and until Pat and I married, he kept giving me little nudges in the direction of other boys.

Especially after Mom died, Daddy had a very rough time trying to care for his three daughters who were still at home. I was in love with Pat. Julie was only thirteen but already had a boyfriend (whom she later married), while Jenny was eleven and still a little girl. Daddy had his hands full!

As I mentioned earlier, Pat was a "careful courter." Therefore, even after he told me that he "thought he loved" me, we didn't begin going steady right away, though we dated continually. One night, however, while Pat was at my house, a boy named Johnny Shea called and asked me for a date.

For my purposes, the call couldn't have been more perfectly timed because Pat and Johnny were natural competitors. For one thing, Johnny went to Father Ryan High School, which was one of Lipscomb's big rivals during baseball and basketball season. Then, too, he was recognized all over Nashville as a good singer, just as Pat was. In other words, Johnny challenged Pat in more ways than one; so, when he called me while Pat was sitting in our living room, I milked that conversation for all it was worth.

I was saying, "Well, Johnny, let me see. Friday night?"—hoping Pat would react, and sure enough he did.

"You tell him," Pat said emphatically, "that *you're going steady!*"

So from that time on we only dated each other, thereby attracting the increasing concern of Pat's parents and, to a certain extent, of my dad.

Daddy was terribly afraid I'd be hurt. But eventually he resumed a social life of his own so that he had less time to worry about mine.

Meanwhile, as my relationship with Pat intensified, my relationship with his church improved. After Mom's death, I felt a great need for God, greater than I'd ever felt before. And since I felt a great need for Pat, I began to accept his religious views. After talking with him about the Church of Christ, I'd think, *Maybe I've been wrong. Maybe it would be pleasing to God if I were baptized again in the Church of Christ. I don't really care what's involved doctrinally, just so I'm closer to Jesus.*

Still, one big stumbling block to my full acceptance of the Church of Christ remained: its doctrine which held that my Baptist mother hadn't been saved. That really hurt me.

But finally I decided that I had to trust my mother to God while at the same time I'd try to do whatever God expected of *me.* Whenever I had a question about God's will, Pat seemed to have an answer. He really knew his Bible. So, reinforced by his assurance that I was doing the right thing, I at long last was baptized again, into the Church of Christ.

About a year after Mom died, Daddy remarried and our family life sort of fell apart. Jenny, the baby, went to live with our married sister, while Julie and I moved in with one of Mom's close friends who lived near Lipscomb.

I guess Pat and I were near the end of our senior year in high school when Mr. and Mrs. Boone, foreseeing so many problems if our romance became more serious, suggested that we not see each other so much. And, because Pat and I respected our parents, we tried hard to please them. But the separation was agony.

Mrs. Evelyn Butler, who'd been a friend of my mother's, tried to make things easier for me by taking me to Florida with her family for a month during the summer. I should have enjoyed a marvelous vacation, but before the end of that month I'd lost twenty-three pounds! Still, I wanted to do what Pat's parents expected of me—stay away from their son for the sake of his future. His future and mine. So, when I got back to Nashville and went over to Lipscomb one summer day to get something, I had no intention of seeing him.

However, quite by accident, we ran into each other.

And, all of a sudden, my stomach was filled with butterflies, my heart was pounding so hard it almost shook me, and all the awful yearning I'd hoped to escape was with me again. Of course, neither Pat nor I knew how to act or what to say, and I, at least, felt guilty as though I'd planned our encounter.

I remember being glad that I'd lost so much weight and had a good tan. Yet, at the same time I wanted to cry because I knew—I was absolutely certain—that things weren't over between Pat and me. And still we couldn't see each other. That being the case, I wanted to get away—as far away from Nashville as I possibly could, because I couldn't risk another accidental meeting. The torment of seeing Pat without being able to date him was more than I could handle. So I went to visit my married sister, Betty, in Kentucky. However, I couldn't stay there forever, and when I got home I ran into Pat again.

Much to Daddy's dismay, I didn't date anybody that whole summer. Daddy kept "matchmaking," trying to get me out with first one boy and then another, but I couldn't scrape up an interest in any of them.

When school started, though, I forced myself to change tactics. Maybe women are naturally conniving, because I quite deliberately set my cap for the most popular boys on campus simply to impress Pat. I thought I'd feel better if he knew that other boys found me attractive.

Still, that didn't help. When Pat and I saw each other with our respective dates at various school events, it was just bad news!

Then, to make matters worse, my Dad said Pat didn't love me. If he did, Daddy said, he'd see me no matter what. Daddy, the same Daddy who'd once rushed to my defense with a pitchfork, was worried about his little girl and was losing patience with the whole situation.

Finally, though, Pat wrote me a letter which I still have and treasure. It's one of the most precious things I've ever read, and when I opened it I knew he loved me after all. I couldn't wait to get home and show it to Daddy.

Then, because love is the most irresistible force in the world, it was inevitable that Pat and I would begin to date again, and we did, though secretly. Daddy knew what we were doing, but he didn't care because by that time he only wanted me to be happy.

Pat and I both felt terrible about deceiving his parents and, actually, we didn't deceive them completely, because a couple of times they found out about our "accidental" meetings. That caused more misunderstandings and hurt feelings.

And then as a horrible climax to our misery, Daddy announced that he was going to move to Springfield, Missouri! He might as well have said Hong Kong!

Earlier I'd thought I wanted to run away from Pat, so I'd gone to my sister's in Kentucky. But by the time Daddy decided to move to Missouri, I knew that leaving Pat would be like leaving my life. I'd tried everything I could think of to forget him, but nothing had worked. I'd even tried dating a Vanderbilt football star, partly because Daddy loved football, but mostly in hopes of escaping my heartache. However, even with a very sweet, good looking, college football star at my side, I was unhappy and lonely.

When Pat and I were together we felt awful, weighed down with guilt, because we were defying his parents. But when we were apart we felt worse. Meanwhile, Mr. and Mrs. Boone must have been suffering too. Pat's unhappiness hurt them. Yet, because they felt their responsibilities as parents, they held to their convictions.

I expect Pat remembered our teenage dilemma when he addressed a group of young people not long ago in Monroe, Louisiana. During a question-and-answer period, a teenage boy asked him how he felt about racially mixed marriages, and Pat answered like this:

"I have four daughters," he said, "and I hope I'm prepared for the possibility that one day one of them will come in and say, 'Daddy, I love George, and George is black....'

"This could very well happen since our kids always have been taught color should make no difference in human relations.

"In such an event, I'd have to tell my daughter and George that they'd have to decide for themselves whether or not to marry—but that in making the decision, they should carefully *count the cost*.

"For, all through life you pay for what you get and what you do. Whether you marry this person or that, whether you dress one way or another, whether you stay in school or drop out—*there's a price tag attached to every choice*. You can't just have things your way and get away without paying the bill.

"Further, when you choose a husband or wife, not only you but your children will pay for your choice! So, before you decide to marry, be sure you understand just what the decision will mean, not only to you but to others."

I think that's more or less what Pat's mother and father were saying to us through their efforts to keep us apart. They were simply urging us not to rush into marriage without fully comprehending the results. And we *were* young—nineteen, both of us.

But as the time for the Foley move to Missouri approached, Dr. Mack Craig, who'd been Pat's high school counselor, teacher, and good friend, realized that Pat and I weren't going to give each other up, so he and his wife helped us elope.

Dr. Craig explained later, "I knew they were going to marry anyway, and I wanted them to have a nice Christian wedding."

Daddy gave his consent before the ceremony, but Mr. and Mrs. Boone didn't know about the wedding until it was over and I was Pat's wife. Naturally, they were shocked. But when Pat brought me home, they greeted me with affection.

As Mrs. Boone held out her arms to me, her eyes filled with tears as she said, "We've tried every way we could to prove you were wrong—and now we'll do everything we can to prove that you're right."

And for the past nineteen years she's been as good as her word.

8

In The Beginning

Talk about blind adoration!

When Pat and I married, I was so much in love I didn't have any sense at all. Pat has said in interviews that we married fully aware of the serious adjustments we'd have to make and the financial crises we'd face, but he was speaking strictly for himself. As far as I was concerned, I wasn't aware of anything except that he was wonderful and that life without him would be miserable.

I understood exactly how Mary, Queen of Scots, must have felt when she said of James Bothwell, her third husband, "I'd follow him to the ends of the earth in my petticoat," because that's how I felt about Pat.

Fortunately, at first I didn't have to follow him any further than to Denton, Texas. Nevertheless, if Pat had suggested it, I would have gone with him to Timbuktu without batting an eye. He was my life. To me, he was perfect, and that was the beginning of our troubles, because anyone placed on a pinnacle can go in only one direction: down.

Nobody's perfect, not even Pat Boone, but it was his misfortune and mine that I didn't realize this for years. Our marriage, according to almost all logical thinking, didn't have a chance in a million to succeed. I'm sure that most objective marriage counselors would have told us to get a divorce immediately before we broke our hearts attempting the impossible. There was no logical way for us to be happy because we'd not only married before we were old enough to assume the responsibilities of a serious relationship, but Pat hadn't completed his education (nor had I completed mine). Pat didn't have a full-time job, we had almost no money, and we were getting entirely too much help and advice from well-meaning friends and relations.

Our situation was impossible. Yet, since we didn't know it, we were idiotically pleased with ourselves. Pat's future was uncertain, to put it mildly, but I never questioned that he'd be able to provide for me. I was sure that, whatever happened, we'd be happy together. Memory of my superb confidence in the days when we scarcely had a dime made my misery the deeper in later years when, living in a big house in Beverly Hills, I thought I'd never love Pat again and wished I were dead.

Material things, however, have never been important to my happiness, so, as a starry-eyed though potentially starving bride, I didn't feel a need for anything more than what I had: Pat Boone.

We set up housekeeping on a modest scale in a little duplex in Nashville. Daddy gave us a redwood sofa and two chairs he'd used by the swimming pool and they furnished our living room. Our coffee table was Pat's barbell bench with a scarf on it, and our end table was a box with a quilt over it that "more or less matched" the sofa.

We set up a card table in the dining room and used a hope chest Daddy gave me as a high school graduation present for storage. I used remnants and Mom's sewing machine to make some valances.

Pat had bought a car from his dad, which we kept so long it became a kind of family heirloom.

As a bride and bridegroom, Pat and I had no luxuries and only barest necessities, but these necessary ingredients included the most important of all to a happy life: love—and a simple childlike religious faith, upon which we agreed. For by that time I'd accepted Pat's religious views almost as completely as I'd accepted everything else about him.

Pat stayed at Lipscomb one semester after we married, but then we declared our independence from everything except God and each other by moving to Denton, Texas and transferring to North Texas State Teacher's College. It had fine music and speech departments, and it was a long way from home!

I'm certain that moving to Texas was one of the smartest things we ever did, because, separated from all else that was dear and familiar, we had to depend upon each other—totally. In case of a quarrel, the only space Pat and I could put between us was the distance between two rooms in our tiny three-room apartment. Any couple in such confined quarters has to patch up differences in a hurry—or learn to share the bathroom!

However, in Denton we had few differences. Because we had a solid faith in God and accepted what we knew of His Word without question, our relationship with each other and the world was sound and happy.

Our move to Denton coincided with a Texas drought, accompanied by wind storms, so much of the time it seemed that we lived encased in dust. Dust was *every*where—in the sink, in the toothpaste, and under the rug. To add to our problems, for a time Pat couldn't get a job; when he finally did find part-time work, it was in Fort Worth and paid only $44.50 a week.

Yet, none of this bothered me. In fact, our months in Denton were some of the sweetest, most precious we've ever known. We not only lived within our budget; we *saved* money! I had a cookbook with a title like "244 Ways to Cook Potatoes," and I tried nearly every one of them. A little country store near us sometimes sold club steaks for a quarter each, and when we could get a couple of those, man, that was our feast! Then, occasionally, for a real treat we'd stop by the local dairy freeze and get a "slush" of some kind.

We couldn't afford a movie, but from time to time one would be shown on the campus at a cut rate in connection with a student talent show. When that happened, Pat usually sang, so we got in free.

We'd arrived in Denton with a little nest egg, some money Pat had saved plus some I'd inherited from my mother, and Pat got the idea that to augment our income we should invest it in chinchillas. We bought a pair, and sure enough, they produced a litter of *five* which, for chinchillas, is about as unusual as it would be if human parents had quintuplets!

Naturally we thought we were going to be rich.

We babied those things almost more than we babied Cherry when she was born. I was putting water in little bottles and putting out alfalfa pellets and cleaning cages as though our future depended upon it.

But, before we realized a fortune from chinchillas, Pat had a hit record, and we got busy with so many other things that we gave them to our friends the Russ Dyers. I don't know what ever became of that first business investment.

One thing we never considered to help our finances was the possibility of Pat dropping out of school to take a full-time job. If he'd done that, his parents' worst fears would have been realized and I would have been a self-admitted failure as a wife. Because, you see, when we married I knew that it was *my* duty as well as his to see that he finished school. His degree was always a definite part of our life plan.

On the other hand, we didn't plan for him to become a professional singer and actor. Not only were his folks against the idea, but when he and I had talked about it we'd agreed that it was no way for him to spend his life. We sort of felt at that time that a professional entertainer didn't contribute anything except momentary pleasure to others and we thought that wasn't enough. We also knew (and had others constantly warning us) of the difficulty of living a Christian life in the entertainment field.

Pat fully expected to be a high school teacher. Meanwhile, he tried to make his contribution to the world by going to church and school and work and by leading a Cub Scout troop.

He has said that he didn't fully commit himself to a career in entertainment until he got to Columbia University and was confronted with an either-or situation. I think though, that I knew he had changed his direction while still in Denton after he had made some records.

Having grown up in a show-business family, I knew how fickle the public can be, so I wasn't sure that Pat would become a major star or that his success would continue. Yet, I began to believe—we both believed—that God must be directing him into the field of entertainment because opportunities in that area came so fast. It was almost as though show business was pursuing *him*, since Pat at that point wasn't pursuing it.

If I sometimes questioned the turn our life was taking, Pat would answer that God must want him to sing and act, or otherwise so many openings wouldn't be coming his way. Occasionally, though, I wasn't sure about that. I wondered, *Could it be Satan?*

Not having been brought up in a church that believes in signs or indications from the Lord, we weren't certain how to interpret the things that were happening to us. All we could do was pray and trust that we were obeying God's will.

Walking in a gray area, where you're not sure what's right and what's wrong, can be very dangerous. Pat, however, could adjust to the grayness better than I. I tended to look for the black and the white of each situation and to be more pessimistic about the outcome. I was more cautious than Pat and more afraid because I'd known the reality of deep pain, which was something he'd never experienced. I think I even loved more deeply than he did, and thus was more vulnerable to hurt.

Still, in our pre-Hollywood days, because we were trying to walk in God's way, we were happy most of the time. And God, recognizing that we wanted to please Him, blessed us.

I remember one particular instance of his protection. Cherry was a baby, and Pat was traveling to promote his first Dot records. Every time he left me, I missed him so much that I'd often hold Cherry throughout her naps just to feel closer to him.

I had the itinerary for the trip he was making at the moment and knew he was supposed to be visiting a television station in Philadelphia. Although Philadelphia isn't normally tornado country, at the very hour Pat was supposed to be there, I heard on the radio that *a tornado had struck a Philadelphia television station,* killing four men and injuring twenty-eight! Naturally I was frantic.

However, God was watching over us. Pat wasn't in Philadelphia after all—he had missed his plane! I firmly believe that, since we were earnestly seeking God at that time, He was protecting us in ways we may never know until we meet Him in heaven.

Before Pat and I were old enough to vote, we'd come through some times of testing. My pregnancy with Cherry was difficult. Then, before Lindy was born, we were told that the baby might be dead.

Pat's hours had been long and our finances short. Nevertheless, we'd survived all of this with our hope and love and awareness of God intact.

It was only after we'd moved into a marble hall (literally) with "all our worries over"—by the world's standards—that we lost everything that meant anything to us, including, in my case, the will to live.

9

Where There's Smoke

Our life, viewed in retrospect, is divided into periods somewhat like a world history book. Instead of being segmented into the Prehistoric period, the Greco-Roman period, the Dark Ages, and the Middle Ages, our personal history divides quite naturally into the Nashville period, the Denton period, the New York-early Hollywood period, the Dark Ages, and the days of victory which came with our baptism by the Holy Spirit.

After Pat began to attract national attention as a singer, we knew we'd have to leave Denton even though we didn't want to. It was a nice town, such a good place to bring up children, that we clung to the notion that perhaps we could settle there permanently.

After Pat's first record for Dot was released, he began to travel a lot while I sat at home, clinging to Cherry and to the idea that our lives might still go on much as before.

However, he was offered a regular spot on "The Arthur Godfrey Show" and we knew we'd have to move into the

New York area and that Pat would have to transfer to a university there.

Still, we told ourselves, three things in our lives would remain constant: Pat's determination to get a degree, our love for each other, and our faith in God.

When we moved to New York, I was pregnant with Lindy and, right in the middle of the packing, I was warned that because I have Rh-negative blood, the baby would probably be born dead!

I flew from Texas to Nashville and Pat joined me for a brief visit with his folks. Pat had to be in New York in a few days to enroll at Columbia University. The baby was due in six weeks, so we decided to go and look for a place to live and enroll him in school.

I tried to take my grief about the baby to God, but I also wanted to be with Pat if I had to bear the heartbreak of losing my child. So I left Cherry in Nashville with Mrs. Boone and went to Manhattan with my husband. A few days later Pat went to Chicago for the weekend.

On Sunday I was alone in my room at the Victoria Hotel when labor began, *four or five weeks early*. I didn't know one soul in the city except a doctor I'd seen there one time.

Since Pat was due back that night, I tried to be calm and delay labor as much as I could by staying in bed. Once settled, I realized that watching television might make the afternoon more bearable, but I wouldn't get up to turn on the set for fear of hurrying the birth.

I thought of Cherry at her grandparents' home, wondered how she was, and missed her. I wondered what Pat was doing and wished mightily that he were with me. And I prayed for the poor little baby who might be entering life only to lose it—the baby who might be in God's presence even before she was in mine.

The hours passed miserably, but finally the phone rang and I heard Pat's voice. He was calling from the airport.

Maybe the first thing I said was, "I'm so glad you're back."

The second thing was definitely, "I think I'm in labor."

Pat took that calmly, which didn't surprise me, because he'd been cool as a cucumber when Cherry was born. But I *was* surprised when he answered, "Have you had anything to eat? Why don't you meet me at church and afterward we'll have dinner."

Church!

Dinner!

It's a measure of how completely I was under Pat's spell that I didn't scream, "Have you gone totally crazy?"

I didn't—and instead, agreed to meet him at church!

It's amazing how forbearing a woman in labor can be. A friend of mine recalls how her husband, en route to the hospital, stopped for a Coke because he said he needed something to perk him up, while she, in hard labor, waited in the car. In fact, he was stunned that she didn't want a Coke too. The husband was still wiping his mouth when they arrived at the hospital—ten minutes before the baby was born!

Well, I met Pat at church, looking almost as bad as I felt. But, if he was concerned that I might give birth in the middle of a hymn, he didn't show it. At that point, I sort of hoped that I would.

After the service we went to a downtown restaurant for soup and, while we were eating, my dearest friend from Chicago and her husband walked by the window and saw us. Naturally they came in for a chat. The four of us had just left the restaurant when my water broke.

Right there on Broadway!

Finally, I think, Pat was convinced of my condition, because he hurried me into a cab and to the hotel and suggested calling the doctor. I was in labor from Sunday until Tuesday when a very yellow, very jaundiced—but living—Lindy was born. After such an ordeal, I was absolutely exhausted, but happier than I'd been in weeks. Our baby was going to be all right after all. God, as usual, had blessed us.

The next year we acquired Debby, and the next, Laury. Meanwhile Pat acquired a television series of his own, gold records, and a motion-picture contract.

Things got so hectic that he was tempted to drop out of school, despite the fact that it would have meant abandoning the one concrete thing we'd always wanted: Pat's diploma.

Keeping his television show going, making records, carrying twenty hours of college classes and trying to be a good father to the girls had become almost more than Pat could manage. So, when exams came, he was just a tiny bit tempted to forget about graduation.

He did drop out of Columbia for one semester during which he went to Hollywood to make the movies *Bernadine* and *April Love.* And in Hollywood, of all places, he got some of the encouragement he needed to go back to school. Or perhaps I should say he was threatened back into classes!

My first trip out to California was a terrifying experience. I knew I wasn't equipped to be the wife of a star and, if I'd been in any doubt, there were plenty of people eager to advise me of my shortcomings. I received nasty letters saying I didn't know how to dress, that I was overweight, and that it was disgraceful for anyone to have so many children so fast. Someone wrote that she'd seen me on television and that I was too ugly to be married to Pat.

Articles hinted (or said) that I was an awkward small-town girl without enough sophistication for the Hollywood scene. As the criticism swept over and around me, my old insecurities returned. I was hurt and afraid.

We'd just read several stories suggesting that Pat was caught in the Hollywood trap, that he'd never go back to school or retain his old values, when we were invited to our first Hollywood party, which was to be given by *Photoplay* magazine. It was to be an awards dinner, with Pat asked to sing in front of some of the biggest stars in the industry. The thought of it not only scared me—it scared him!

But we went and he sang "Anastasia" and "Friendly Persuasion." And, though nobody asked who'd designed my gown, everyone was kind and friendly. To my surprise, I actually enjoyed myself and, when I was introduced to Doris Day, I felt quite giddy.

However, we owe the most memorable moment of the evening to Kirk Douglas, who confronted Pat with a clenched fist and said, "If you don't finish school, I'm going to come after you and personally clobber you."

Pat was taller than Kirk, but that famous Douglas chin with its attractive cleft, and those famous Douglas teeth (clenched), and those famous Douglas eyes (blazing) were so overpowering that Pat hurriedly assured Kirk, "Don't worry. I'm planning on it."

Pat *was* planning to go back to school anyway, but I've always appreciated the nudge Kirk Douglas gave him.

Like all couples, Pat and I had had occasional differences throughout our marriage, but while he was attending Columbia we had our first serious disagreement that stemmed—though indirectly—from his career.

He was working so hard away from school that he sometimes had trouble staying awake during classes. So one day he came home with a pipe! My parents smoked, and I'd never felt it was *wrong*. After gaining so much weight having my first two babies, I decided smoking might help me lose weight! I smoked for about a week, but when Pat came to me and said, "Seeing you with a cigarette in your mouth bothers me. You're just not the same girl I married," I immediately gave it up.

Previously Pat had been violently opposed to using tobacco in any form, so I was amazed when he brought home the pipe. But then he explained that smoking a pipe was different than smoking cigarettes because with a pipe you didn't inhale and take the poisons into your system. I call this Pat's "gift of rationalization." When he explained these differences and said this might help keep him awake at school, I accepted his logic.

Pretty soon, though, he began smoking cigars as well as his pipe, until the house absolutely reeked with fumes. He loved the aroma, but to me it was so offensive it literally made me sick. Unsuccessfully I used his own argument on him, "Honey, you're just not the guy I married."

It didn't faze him! This really hurt me, because I now felt he didn't love me—judging him on *my* scale of "how to love."

Finally I told him, "If you want to smoke, that's your business; but please don't do it around me. I hate it." We bickered about this for years, with me throwing in an occasional, "You're ruining your image." Pat, you see, had participated in antismoking campaigns in the schools, so the sight of a pipe or cigar in his mouth was hypocritical to me.

One day a friend of ours from church, who'd heard Pat speak out against smoking, came to our house and saw the big pipe rack. He was disappointed by the double standard and deeply concerned. And I was embarrassed beyond words. Pretty soon, though, the words came back and I directed them all at Pat, berating him more than ever about his habit.

Now I know my fault was as grievous as his. More grievous. For I'd not only forgotten my marriage vow to honor my husband, I'd also forgotten the scriptural admonition: "Judge not that you be not judged."

I was filled with two ugly emotions: pride in my own righteousness, and anger at Pat's lack of it.

At that time I hadn't become convinced that God *really expects submission* from wives, so with anger and arrogance I nagged my husband. If, after seemingly going from one problem right into another, I hadn't come into a new relationship with God through the baptism with the Holy Spirit, I'd probably be nagging yet—provided Pat were around to listen.

However, after I'd surrendered myself completely to God, I learned that if I also surrendered all daily aggravations to Him, the Lord would take care of them in His own way and time. So I said no more to Pat about tobacco.

One day, as I was packing his suitcase for a trip, I saw a box of cigars and asked him, "Are you taking these?"

He said that he was and asked me to put them in the lower part of his duffel bag. At one time I would have started an argument right then and there, but content in my new relationship with God, I carefully packed the box without comment.

I just prayed, "Lord, I'm not going to bicker, because maybe I'm making too big a deal out of this thing. But, if You'd rather that Pat not be smoking these smelly things, even privately, please get rid of his cigars."

About a week later I was packing for Pat again and came across another box of cigars.

Again I asked, "Honey, are you taking these?"

He said, "Yes, but don't pack them the way you packed the last ones. When I opened my duffel bag, the box was completely demolished—there wasn't one cigar I could smoke."

At that, I had to sit down and chuckle silently.

Lord, I thought, *why didn't I ask You to take over a long time ago?*

Pat didn't take his mashed cigars as any sign from God, but to me they carried a direct message: "Shirley, you leave him alone, and I'll take care of his desire to smoke."

So after that I never said another word to Pat about his smoking, but from time to time I'd go to the cabinet in which he kept his expensive cigars and tobacco and pray that they wouldn't tempt him.

One night about four of us prayed that Pat would be relieved of the appetite for tobacco, trusting in God to erase the desire. For two years nothing happened, and I mean *nothing.* Since I'd quit nagging Pat about smoking, we didn't even argue about his cigars. One night, though, while we were praying with a group in our family room, Pat suddenly jumped up, disappeared, and then came back with a rack of about thirty fantastically expensive pipes and *threw them into the fire.*

He said that as we'd been praying it had occurred to him that smoking was bad for his voice and that, if he were going to use his voice for God, he'd have to sacrifice his beloved habit.

Immediately a friend announced that Pat had "sinned" by burning those pipes which might have been given to a veterans' hospital. She didn't say it to me, but I overheard her telling my brother-in-law that burning the pipes had been like burning money.

I thought, *Was it a sin? Should we have sold the pipes and donated the proceeds to a Christian college?* But then I remembered that Pat had acted on impulse which came to him while he was in prayer. I remember how the apostle had rebuked Mary for anointing Jesus' feet with costly ointment which might have been sold for the benefit of the poor—and I remembered how Jesus had *commended* her! [1] So I concluded that since Pat had burned his pipes to honor God without thinking about their monetary value, the act was between my husband and my Lord, and not between my friend and anybody.

A few days later, Pat had his birthday, and in our family it's our custom for the person who's celebrating the birthday to *give* gifts instead of the other way around. Since it's more blessed to give than to receive, we look forward with unusual joy to birthdays.

On Pat's birthday during dinner, he turned to me and said, "Honey, I have something for you that you've always wanted."

Then he went upstairs and brought down two wastebaskets full of expensive pipes and cigars. We put them in the fireplace and made a great big blaze with all that rich tobacco. As the smoke went up the chimney, Pat went into the yard for a few final sniffs and reported that the entire neighborhood smelled fabulous!

I don't condemn people for smoking, but I believe that God wanted Pat to give it up. Besides, smoking damages our bodies which are temples for the Holy Spirit and should be treated with care. [2]

Recently many people have given up smoking for health rather than for religious reasons, but when Pat gave it up he was foregoing something he truly enjoyed in order to glorify God, and I think that was an action of special worth.

Since Pat quit smoking, he says his voice is better and that he no longer has any desire for tobacco. Further, he's devoting the many minutes he used to spend each day smoking—to prayer. He says he hadn't realized it before, but his pipes and cigars had been cutting into his prayer time. Without them, he has more leisure to enjoy something much sweeter than any tobacco blend—a closer contact with and refreshment from the Lord.

How I wish, looking back, that all our problems and major differences could have been handled so painlessly. But it wasn't to be.

Our Dark Ages were almost upon us.

10
The Misfit

At first setting up housekeeping in Hollywood was a Tom Sawyer and Huck Finn adventure for Pat and me.

I learned later that a very nice publicist who helped find our first Hollywood house was nervous the day we arrived because he was sure we wouldn't like the mansion he rented for us. But actually, though it didn't seem real to us and had a few drawbacks as a residence for young children, we were rather pleased with his choice.

The floor was partially marble, and statues in the entrance hall seemed more appropriate for a museum than a home. Further, the house had a high balcony which might have been fatally enticing to toddlers. However, Pat and I licked that hazard by stringing chicken wire along the balustrade so that not even our most daring daughter could plunge over.

The statues became subjects of family jokes; for, though Pat was now a movie star and one of the top attractions at the nation's box offices, we still didn't have a twelve-foot banquet table, a staff of servants, or other luxuries appropriate to a house of that kind.

We were still just Tennessee corn bread and turnip greens folk, agog at the Hollywood grandeur, and secretly suspecting that we'd wake up after a while and find we'd been dreaming.

Even so, that house with its great stairway furnished a beautiful setting for my youngest sister's wedding, making us happy that we lived there so she could use it.

In fact, Pat finally became so attached to the place that he wanted to buy it. But, as I recall, it wasn't for sale—and after we left, Elvis Presley moved in.

Unfortunately, though, not everything in Hollywood was as easy for me to adjust to as was the house with its statues. I could laugh at the elaborate decor, but I couldn't laugh at all of the other novelties which were creeping into our lives.

Abe Lincoln said, "If you look for the bad in mankind, be prepared to find it," and, remembering that, I valiantly determined to look for only the best as I encountered new situations. Further, I reminded myself, since it seemed to be God's will that Pat have a career in show business, I probably shouldn't criticize the environment in which we'd been placed.

As a young girl, I'd found it easy to overlook the shortcomings of others, and so, once I'd gotten over my own terrible inferiority complex, I'd enjoy happy associations with most of the people I met. In Hollywood, however, I was beginning to let my old insecurities slip back in magnified form. Even at the *Photoplay* party, where people were as cordial as could be, I felt totally out of place. I know I judged myself more harshly that night than anybody else did, for, even though my dress may not have been high fashion, I'm sure others were sympathetically thinking, "They're young. They've just moved here. They're sort of cute."

Yet, the sense of self-worth I'd developed at West and Lipscomb was gradually being replaced by recurring guilt pangs. I was so supercritical of myself—my figure, my lack of fashion sense, my unworthiness to be Pat's wife—that I could scarcely believe that anyone—even God—could love me.

I needed desperately to feel needed, but Pat had never been one to display his emotions much, so he didn't give me enough of the reassurance I hungered for. He was much too self-reliant. I began to look forward to times when Pat would be sick, because then at least I knew that he needed me. But unfortunately (or fortunately) he's one of the healthiest men alive, so he wasn't sick often.

My mounting sense of self-condemnation combined with my natural maternal instinct began to cut me off from people who were Pat's new friends and, in turn, to cut me off from Pat. I judged others as harshly as I judged myself and asked Pat not to associate with those who, I felt, would be bad influences on the girls. As a result, we didn't entertain on a large scale, and when we went to parties I was obviously ill at ease.

The people we met in Hollywood weren't the only ones who disappointed me. So did Pat. During those years, I searched my heart and prayed hard that God would guide me in my relationship with my husband, that I wouldn't be unreasonably prudish. Nevertheless, I felt that by making certain moral compromises we were opening the door to problems we might not be able to handle.

When Pat made *April Love* with Shirley Jones, the fact that they didn't kiss was widely publicized. In fact, it was reported and believed that Pat hadn't kissed Shirley because I wouldn't let him. That story wasn't true, because one moral decision Pat didn't have to make at that stage in his career was whether or not he'd kiss his leading lady.

No kiss had been in the *Bernadine* script, nor was one in the script for *April Love,* so for a long time we didn't even consider how I'd feel when and if he had to play a love scene. We were a couple of very naïve kids who'd met under romantic circumstances in a church school and who hadn't weighed all the aspects of movie-making until it became a part of our lives.

Anyway, while *April Love* was being filmed one day, Pat was asked by the director to kiss Shirley Jones. It was an unexpected request, and he said, "Gee, I don't know. I'd like to talk to Shirley (me) about it." No kissing scene was ever written into the picture, but Pat's reaction made international headlines.

Confronted with all the controversy over whether or not Pat should have kissed Shirley Jones (now our good friend), I had to ask myself how I'd feel when he *might* do love scenes in movies. He and I talked about it, and I told him, "I can't say now exactly how I'll react, but I *do* know it will bother me. I wouldn't be normal if it didn't. On the other hand, honey, I can adjust to it . . . just as a doctor's wife has to adjust to the fact that her husband examines women all day. It's his work.

"Still, I can't pretend I'll enjoy it. Put yourself in my position and think how you'd feel if the circumstances were reversed and I spent the afternoon kissing Rock Hudson!"

When Pat did that, he had to admit that he wouldn't like for me to kiss Rock Hudson, even though I might argue, "It's just a job. It means no more than kissing a wall."

Maybe the trouble was that we were too young and our marriage wasn't as stable as we'd thought. Otherwise, a screen kiss might not have mattered. However, at that time Pat realized as well as I that there were some compromises we should make only after much prayerful consideration, or never make at all.

When Pat finally *did* kiss a girl on screen, she was Diane Baker, and their kiss in *Journey to the Center of the Earth* was so innocent that I didn't mind it. Hardly anybody noticed it. After that, though, his love scenes became more and more torrid, leading up, at last, to a picture called *The Main Attraction* which appalled me.

Pat was making that picture in England when, pregnant for the fifth time, I was so unhappy that I begged God to take our unborn baby. As Pat has described in his book, *A New Song,* God answered my prayer. I didn't learn whether the baby would have been a boy or a girl, but I did learn that it would probably have been abnormal.

I miscarried during an agony-filled period in my life, though not the most unhappy I would know. Worse months and years were ahead. For Pat and I were disagreeing now on so *many* subjects!

When he began singing in Las Vegas, I was against it. He went places, did things and associated with people I didn't like and, as a result, I was constantly wracked by warring emotions. I felt that Pat was turning his back on me and our daughters and upon the Lord as we had known Him. I wanted to stay close to God, but at the same time I still felt protective toward Pat. I'd about given up hope that he would leave the path he was following, so the hope I finally clung to was: "Maybe nobody will know."

Yet, so long as God and I knew, there was no peace for me.

At last, after years of emotional conflict, my body reacted with collapse. Doctors said I had mononucleosis, but I was suffering more from spiritual near-defeat.

I was in a coma three days. I lost twenty pounds in twelve days. While I was in the coma, I wasn't totally unconscious, for I could hear people coming in and out of my room and whispering. I was aware of arms and legs on my bed, but I couldn't move my body. I felt as though I were removed from the woman lying so quietly, as though I were a witness in a far corner of the room looking at myself. It was a weird experience.

Then, on the third day of the coma, I had a clear and frightening vision. I saw a fiery chariot coming for the prostrate Shirley, peopled by little demonic creatures, and I was sure Satan had asked for me.

Terrified? I was more afraid than I'd ever been in my life. I thought, *This is it. Here I go. Satan wants me.*

But that thought made me fight back, so that during the night or early the next morning I came out of the coma. Still, three days of my life were irrevocably gone.

I rolled off my bed and crawled to the telephone to call the only person I knew who, I thought, would understand my experience and pray for me and not try to put me into a mental institution. I asked him to call a couple of women we knew who believed in demonic activity and ask them to pray for me too, which they did.

Taken to a hospital, I stayed there three weeks, undergoing every kind of test imaginable and mystifying physicians who couldn't find anything wrong enough with me to be causing such damage to my body. Finally they concluded that my difficulties must be partly psychological, so they asked whether I'd mind talking with a psychiatrist. Well, the idea of a psychiatrist turned me off instantly, but I thought, *All right, Shirley, if you honestly want to get well, you should be willing to accept psychiatric treatment.*

Meanwhile, I'd already been getting help from the greatest psychiatrist of all, our Lord. In the hospital I had prayed continuously until I *knew* that God was as close to me as my nurse. Closer. Because He never left the room.

At that time I didn't know about the baptism of the Holy Spirit, but I did know that God was a literal presence, sheltering me with love.

Sometimes I'd have conversations with Him as informal and trusting as I might have had with my earthly father. I'd ask, "Lord, while I sleep for a while, will You please just stand in the room. Please just stay with me." Then I'd go to sleep, knowing that He was there.

I didn't have as much knowledge as I should have had about the Lord and His Holy Spirit, but God knew my heart and knew that, while I'd fallen into dark, earthly traps, I'd always wanted to please Him. So, for the time being, He sheltered and saved me.

It was night when the psychiatrist visited me for the first time, and that in itself unnerved me. I'm naturally a day person. I don't function as well in darkness, and a hospital at night is especially eerie.

The psychiatrist asked me a series of very personal questions which I tried to answer truthfully—all except one. That was about Pat and, because I was still extremely protective toward him, I hedged some. The doctor imagined that we were involved in some kind of triangle, and I'm sure my reaction to his question convinced him of it. Actually, there was no triangle, but Pat and I had other critical problems I wanted to cover up.

Finally the psychiatrist said, "Mrs. Boone, I can't find the source of your problem, but if you really want to know what's the matter with you, why don't you let me hypnotize you?"

I'd been hypnotized before, and the episodes had been most unpleasant. I'd felt myself in danger under hypnosis. So I told the doctor I'd rather not try it again.

"I don't like things I don't understand," I said.

But he continued to reason with me, explaining that if I truly wanted to get well I should submit myself to any medically approved form of treatment. Finally I agreed to his suggestion.

Evidently I'm a very fast subject, because the psychiatrist held a little pen over my eyes and, almost at once, I was reacting.

He said, "All right, now, Mrs. Boone, you see a television screen." And immediately that's what I saw.

He said, "There are pictures on the screen. Please describe them to me."

So I did. I told him I saw people running to and fro, though "to and fro" isn't a phrase I'd normally use. To me, it's scriptural phrasing.

Then the doctor asked me, "Why are the people running?"

I told him I could see them rushing and scrambling, and I knew they were frightened.

When he asked me why they were frightened, I told him I didn't know.

So he asked, "Do you see an answer to their fright?"

And I said, "Yes, Jesus Christ."

After that, he brought me out of the hypnotic state.

I also was given various drugs to put me into a subliminal state in which I could answer questions but not deceive, because doctors were still confused about the root of my illness. Under the drugs, at a time when my reflexes had to be totally honest, I was so close to God that I was blessing everybody. Every time anyone stuck me with a needle, I'd smile and say, "God bless you."

Now this was quite foreign to my conscious nature, because normally I'm not an extrovert. I might normally have said a silent prayer for someone, but I wouldn't have said out loud, "God bless you." But in the hospital, with my inhibitions erased, I was praying aloud for *everyone* with whom I came in contact.

I knew that one of my doctors, Dr. Newman, had a patient in the hospital suffering from what had been diagnosed as a gangrenous pancreas, and I knew that the doctor was terribly concerned about him. Because I loved Dr. Newman, I began to feel strong compassion for this other patient whom I'd never seen in my life and to pray earnestly for him.

In fact, I told Dr. Newman, "If you'll let me know exactly when you are going to perform surgery, I'd like to pray at that time."

Well, Dr. Newman told me, and as he operated, I prayed.

That afternoon while I was in therapy, my therapist was called to the phone. When she came back, she said, "That was Dr. Newman. He asked me to tell you that your prayers have been answered."

I've never met the man who inspired such compassion within me, but my doctor told me later, "Your prayers are the reason he's alive today."

My stay in the hospital brought me closer to God than I'd ever been before. I knew I was in His keeping and that, through His power, all things are possible. So it's hard to explain why, after such closeness as that, I could eventually not only turn my back on God's will, but, in the lowest moment of my life, deny my relationship with Him to one who needed His help.

But that's exactly what I did.

11
Soul In Tatters

To live in terror is to live in hell on earth, and such was my life for approximately seven years.

I was afraid for the future of my marriage. I was afraid for the fate of Pat's soul and, toward the end of my ordeal, I was afraid that I was losing my mind and would lose my children.

In describing the circumstances which created my hell, I may seem to place too much blame on Pat. However, I know that I fell just as short of God's expectations as he did—as we all do in one way or another.

Maybe Pat sinned one time more than I did or I sinned once more than he. But no matter. It's so silly to try to tally one person's sins against another's or to try to balance good deeds against evil. *For a single sin* (and there's nobody on earth who hasn't committed more than that) *completely separates man from God until God's grace redeems him.*

Pat's first Las Vegas booking was an episode typical of many which, through the friction they generated, almost ground our marriage to bits. When he told me he'd been offered a booking there, I begged him not to take it and he said he wouldn't. But then, suddenly, he changed his mind, and the rationalizing began.

He compared Las Vegas to the midway at the Tennessee State Fair, with everything from harmless rides to girl shows and games of chance, offering diversified entertainment for the whole family. Further, Pat argued, Las Vegas needed a clean show, which was true. Yet I knew he wasn't going there simply to bring wholesome joy to the Strip.

His rationalization scared me because it was part of a dangerous pattern I was watching evolve, a design for living which in the past had been totally foreign to Pat. Reluctantly I went with him to Nevada where, to my sick dismay, I not only saw him associating with people who shocked me but I saw him enjoying their company. I heard him tell stories which were not Pat Boone—not the Pat I loved, anyway. I watched him gamble in a small way, and the spectacle tore me to shreds.

Nobody imagined what I was suffering, because only I knew what Pat was really all about. So only I could have suffered the particular torture I was enduring. I tried to be cool, to show my disapproval of what he was doing in subtle ways without shaking an accusing finger in his face. But, I've never been good at hiding my true feelings from Pat. He might choose to ignore my feelings but he knew how I felt.

After a show I'd say, "Well, honey, stay up if you want to, but I'm going back to our room."

No nagging, really; just disgusted silence. But after a time, seeing my forbearance didn't work, I resorted to accusation. I did, figuratively at least, shake my finger in his face and warn him that he was on a disaster course.

All I accomplished by that was to widen the breach between us. If I said, "Don't do something," it almost seemed to challenge Pat. Sort of a "Don't tell me how to live my life" attitude.

When my sisters and Pat's sister came to visit us in Vegas and he wanted to take them to shows, I hung back. I told them they'd have to go without me, whereupon even my own sisters and sister-in-law thought I was too prudish.

"Who does Shirley think she is?" was the general reaction. I was sticking out from the group like a sore thumb and, to tell you the truth, I wasn't even sure I was right. Still the Las Vegas shows offended me. I couldn't comfortably listen to the jokes in the lounges or enjoy other facets of the entertainment, and I was wounded because Pat and the others could.

I fought Pat on so many levels for so many years that our marriage began to sicken. Fatally, it seemed. From time to time, I'd sit down beside him and try to convince him (and myself, I guess) how much I loved him. I'd tell him that I didn't want his career to become a source of contention between us and that, if he really believed his appearances in Vegas served some high purpose, I wouldn't object, but that watching the direction in which he'd been moving, I was concerned and frightened.

By this time Pat was drinking a little bit, not seriously, not any more than he was gambling in a large way, but by drinking and gambling he was playing with fire. Though I had been brought up in a home where there was nothing wrong with dancing, smoking and drinking—at least they were not considered sins—when I started dating Pat, I gave up dancing because I loved him. Later smoking—because I loved him. Now I reminded Pat of this and asked him to please give up Las Vegas "just because you love me."

Again this argument didn't work. He said even if he were to give up his career and become a *minister*, I'd still find something wrong with it.

Maybe he was right at the time, but not now!

I simply couldn't be a part of the life he enjoyed on the Strip, so the next time he accepted a Las Vegas engagement, I refused to stay there with him. I told him, "Look, I'm your wife, and I love you, so I'll go to your opening. I want to stand behind you, but I can't endorse Las Vegas."

So I flew over for Pat's opening night—and then flew home.

Before we got our solid grip on God, Pat's stays in Las Vegas were times of torment for me and temptation for him. I knew that show girls (and other women too) threw themselves at him, because this had happened right in front of my eyes when some girls failed to realize I was Pat's wife. So, remembering that, I hated for him to be in Las Vegas without me. At home, thinking of Pat in another state surrounded by beautiful girls, I was miserable. But I knew if I were with him, watching the beautiful girls, I'd still be miserable and I'd make him miserable too. My marriage would profit more, I decided, if I kept my misery out of his sight. Also my attitude by now was "What you don't know won't hurt you."

I was so exhausted through worry that I was skin and bones. Anyone who saw me must have known I was unhappy because it was written all over my face. I couldn't play games, which was a virtue of sorts but one which made my very presence a reproach to Pat.

But what great changes have taken place in the past few years! We've been through a wonderful teaching process. We needed to learn many lessons before we could accomplish God's purpose for us in Las Vegas. Where Pat had made his decisions before based on an entertainer's values—now he sees Vegas as an opportunity to reach souls *that might never set foot in a church!*

Now our daughters and I perform with Pat in Las Vegas as a family, and I not only don't mind, I *enjoy* it. But our motivation is quite different from what Pat's was years back. Now we know that we can glorify God anywhere, including a casino showroom, and that He can use us in unexpected ways and places.

But before this "great change," whenever Pat was in Los

Angeles, I went to parties with him, trying to understand that his own nature and the nature of the business he was in made a social life important.

Pat is naturally friendly, which is part of his charm. In addition, he felt that it was important for him to meet and mingle with top people in the entertainment industry. So, at parties, he was an impulsive table-hopper. There was nothing wrong with that in itself, because I understand the necessity of getting to know every aspect of a person's profession. However, Pat's motivation was wrong, because at that point his interest in our fellow partygoers was at least partially selfish.

I worried about that for a while. And then I didn't worry anymore. By degrees I began to wonder whether *I* was the one who was wrong, the square peg in the round hole, who was a misfit through her own stupid choice.

Looking over a Hollywood party crowd, I'd reason, *You're not the only one in this room who professes to be a Christian. These other people do too, yet they're smoking and drinking, and they think Pat's great. Everybody loves Pat. You're the one nobody likes, so there must be something wrong with you!*

When I began to think like that, the devil had me right where he wanted me. However, I didn't succumb to the devil's enticement without one last flurry of resistance.

Up to that point I had been critical of Pat privately, but I didn't share my concern with others. In the face of the world, I was protective. But now, feeling my own resolution beginning to falter, I talked with our minister about our problems. For Pat's sake and mine, I felt I *had* to ask someone to help me find the right answers.

The minister couldn't help me though, and neither could the elders of the church when I asked them to talk to Pat. They gave advice and showed concern, but it just didn't change anything. They did all they knew to do, but this battle needed power that none of us had plugged into at this point.

So, with that hope having failed me, I felt that the game was up. If our minister and our elders couldn't change Pat, I wondered, how could *I* expect to? Unfortunately I didn't lay the burden directly before the Lord because, you see, *I'd subconsciously made Pat my god.* That was my overwhelming sin.

When he opened at the Coconut Grove, I was there. But throughout the engagement, after his show, I'd sit sleepless in bed waiting for him to come home while he joined first one party and then another, meeting people and accepting congratulations. Every night somebody would distract him so that he'd be late coming home.

One night we played an hysterical scene, like something out of a poorly written movie. Someone had given Pat a bottle of liquor which had broken in his suitcase, so, tiptoeing upstairs, shoes in hand, he smelled like a distillery.

Our arguments began to fall into grooves, with Pat often reminding, "I was only nineteen years old when we married. People change. They should. They have to grow up."

To which I'd answer, "OK, so I'm an immature imbecile. But something's happened. Something's *missing,* and we have to change while there's time." I knew he was thinking, *She's what needs to change!*

In the midst of this kind of life, I was glad to hear that I had mononucleosis. I thought with gratitude, *Now I can just lie down and die.* I was too weary to fight with my husband anymore.

My illness really was a much-needed reprieve during which I got back in close touch with God. However, it was only a small island of solace in the midst of a sea of storms and troubles ready to drown me as soon as I plunged into it again.

God would have seen me through anything if only I'd stayed on my knees, but after my health returned I began to fight for Pat using only human resources. Oh, what a mistake that was! And a companion mistake—or sin—was my indulgence in self-pity. At first I'd centered my concern upon Pat. My inner cry had been, *Look what Pat's doing to himself.* But now I began to think only of Shirley: *Look what Pat's doing to me.* And with that I started a long, fast spiritual fall right into the devil's domain.

Because Pat isn't by nature a sly or devious person, he supplied me with plenty of fuel to fire my self-pity—letters and pictures I accumulated and kept in an envelope to use for my own protection should I eventually need it. In my feverish fancies, I looked toward a terrible day when I might lose not only Pat but my children.

Everybody loves Pat Boone, I repeatedly thought. *He, not I, would get the girls if anything irrevocable happens.* So I clung to my envelope, brooding over the uses to which I could put it should I ever find myself totally threatened.

Because of the attitude I'd developed toward Pat, I was sinning more deeply everyday. I was judging him—and I was jealous.

And I felt good. With my new clothes and hairstyle, I was fighting for my man, and since compliments were giving me confidence, I was beginning to think I'd win everything I wanted.

However, what I was literally doing was destroying myself and my marriage. For, by making gowns, jewels and the games people play at Hollywood parties my chief concern, I was in effect saying, "God, I want Pat more than I want You."

Also as I responded to the praise of others, my head was turned and I forgot biblical admonition, "Pride goeth before destruction" (Proverbs 16:18).

How true that admonition is, I soon found out.

12
Cry In The Darkness

It's both funny and sad to watch a couple at a Hollywood cocktail party exchange a kiss.

Two people, often no more than casual acquaintances, throw themselves at one another with happy, welcoming cries.

Each may be trying to remember the other's name. Each may be wondering whether a kiss is really necessary and, if so, who should initiate it. Wariness underlies the enthusiasm. Yet, in keeping with the ritual, a cheek is tentatively extended. Lips are tentatively pursed and, with a great outward show of affection—the kiss is accomplished.

It's more casually given than a handshake. In most cases, it means absolutely nothing; yet cocktail party kissing is a family-rooted Hollywood tradition, something one must do to be in fashion.

It's like the life-style I adopted in my campaign to recapture Pat—shallow, conforming and unfulfilling.

Having decided to accept Hollywood on its own terms, I

found my life as empty of real satisfaction as a cocktail party kiss is of commitment. Flitting from social event to social event, I congratulated myself upon having mastered the skills and techniques necessary to acceptance.

OK, *Shirley,* I thought, *you too, can wear the frosted hair and jewels and fit into any of the parties where the burning question is, "Who's got something for me?" You don't have to be a misfit anymore. In fact, you can be just like everyone else.*

And quite quickly I was.

I need something. What's in it for me? That was the driving philosophy I constantly encountered and at last adopted. That was what life was all about.

Still, I didn't feel closer to Pat and I wasn't happy, for my subconscious was protesting, trying to draw me back into my former way of life. Sometimes, in fact, even my conscious mind balked at the compromises I was making. One minute I'd want very deeply to run back to the safety of the principles I'd abandoned, but the next minute I wouldn't care what I'd forsaken or which way I was going.

Finally, fed up with the charades but still too hungry for Pat's approval to abandon them, I reached the point where I just didn't care—with the result that I, too, began to drink a little. First came a "little wine" at parties. And I'd like to emphasize there's nothing intrinsically wrong with that. Christ's first miracle was to change water to wine. I personally believe this is an individual decision that must be made, based on a total balance of the Scriptures along with proper motives, and other reasons.

However, anything which impairs your self-control should be avoided, whether it's wine consumed without moderation or other influences in your life which lack scriptural approval and discipline. Wine, I discovered, is an innocent-seeming seducer. So pretty in the glass, so pleasantly relaxing, it produces a false sense of well-being. Sipping it at a party one night, I suddenly realized, *Hey, this isn't so bad.*

This glass is a great little pain killer.

After that, I didn't sip wine to be sociable. I accepted it as a crutch. A glass of wine said to me, "Now you won't have to *think* so much."

With my discretion blunted, I tried other drinks. Drinking didn't seem wrong anymore, because, with each step you take toward darkness, the next grows easier. In darkness, you can't see the pit ahead.

I came to understand, thank God, how Pat had succumbed to Hollywood's trap. Yet, even this understanding wasn't healing my marriage, which was in worse condition, if possible, than it had ever been.

Pat, I was sure, didn't love me, and by that time I didn't think God did either. I couldn't blame God for not loving me, but Pat—oh, how I still wanted him. By this time, the longing came mostly from wounded pride, though I didn't realize it for a while.

Now, everything was gone. My marriage—my faith—all that I'd valued.

Previously, when I'd feared I was losing Pat, I could turn to God and thank Him for being with me though everyone else had turned away. But approaching my deepest agony, I felt that my Lord, as well as my husband, had rejected me.

Some nights when Pat was away from home, I'd go down into the den and fall on my knees, sobbing. Sometimes I'd literally cry out into the lonely silence, "Jesus, please be with me! Do something. *Help me!"*

And Jesus heard, though I didn't think so at the time. By letting me suffer, He tried to warn me, "Shirley, you're on the wrong track. Please come back to *My* way."

Kneeling, weeping, hopeless—I thought I was losing my mind.

One night I sank to the extreme depths of error. An actor, famous for his brittle wit, allowed me the briefest look at the man beneath the veneer. And I failed to give him the response he needed. He challenged, "Aren't you religious?" I'm sure he was hoping I'd say that I was and explain to him why. But instead I answered, "Pat is—"

What a chance I'd been given to affirm my faith and, perhaps, share it with another seeking soul. By my silence, like Peter, I denied Jesus and denied a fellow human being my Christian concern.

When the words were out of my mouth, I could hardly believe I'd said them. What had possessed me? The answer was obvious: Satan.

I'd never believed that I could fall so far. Over and over I seemed to hear Peter answering the question, "Aren't you one of His followers?" with a frightened, "No, not me. *I don't know Him at all!*" (Matthew 26:69-75).

In my self-centered search for love, I had fallen into disobedience and sin. Gorged on pride and self-pity, I'd separated myself from God and been rewarded with heartbreak. While I'd been pursuing the "beautiful people" and their praise, my family life had disintegrated—and, in the last desperate analysis, so had my love for Pat.

That was the real shocker: to comprehend at last, that while I'd clawed and fought for his approval, using "love" as an alibi for all I'd done, my genuine love for him had withered in the same way as my faith.

I still loved my children, but now not even they brought me joy. I played the role of "good mother" only through duty.

Finally, because I could find no earthly consolation, I went all alone to church one Wednesday night and there, before the congregation and God, confessed my sins and gave my life to the Lord.

I had nothing to offer God except myself—so messed up I

wasn't sure He'd want me. I told Him I'd made such a mess of my life that I couldn't stand it unless He took over and straightened it out.

Could even a loving Father make use of a life like mine? Yes. On my knees I knew that He could love and use even the most unlovely of His children. Jesus never condemned people. He said, "Go, and sin no more." Then, loving them as He did, He showed them a better way.

From that night in church, I too, turned around and was given an upward direction. Still my transformation wasn't instantaneous and complete. I'd told God that I was giving Him my life, but, in my spiritual ignorance, I was slow to surrender all my *difficulties.*

For example, because in the marriage ceremony I'd vowed before God to spend my life with Pat, I was resigned to keeping the vow. But I was convinced I would never love my husband again.

In a little while, though, I had enough sense to take the problem to God, and He solved it!

On my knees, I told the Lord how I felt, how I'd never told Pat that I didn't love him anymore—but that I didn't—and that, since I knew *God* loved Pat, I prayed that He'd love him through me.

Well, as I prayed, warm emotion stirred within me. Pat wasn't going to be my god again, something he shouldn't have been in the first place, but, thanks to Jesus, he was going to become my deeply beloved husband.

Through prayer I'd taken a step in that direction.

However, I made my full return to happy marriage *only when I burned my envelope of pictures and notes,* the shabby "evidence" of what I thought were Pat's flirtations I'd been holding to use in self-defense.

I was burning the bridge to *any* future life of my own, apart from Pat. The act of destroying that envelope was nearly as significant in my spiritual development as was my baptism. Because it said to God, "You can see I mean business. My future as a wife, like all my future, is in Your hands."

Gradually God gave me back a love for Pat that is deeper and greater than it had ever been and, simultaneously, renewed Pat's love for me. Oh, we still have disagreements, and in future chapters I discuss some of them. But our marriage is stronger than ever, our happiness more perfect.

When I consider my time of tears and testing, I realize I should praise God for it, because I think He let me endure it for a reason. Having fallen so low myself, *I've learned tolerance.*

I'm sure in the past Pat and I erred by judging others. We looked accusingly at people who were already so full of guilt feelings that they couldn't care less about our judgment. When you're aching with guilt, you don't even feel the stone cast by a self-righteous judge.

Since discovering how wonderfully God could love me in my most unlovely conditions, *I've been able to love more people.* It's a shame all of us can't see the truth without falling flat on our faces, but some of us need a hard lesson before we perceive the graciousness of God.

After I asked the Lord to take charge of my life, Pat and the girls noticed a change in me. I was happier—as I should have been, with my focus off myself and relieved of so much guilt.

Reading my Bible regularly and praying earnestly, I learned more every day about God. And, as part of the learning process, I became increasingly aware of a Member of the Trinity I'd never thought much about before—the Holy Spirit.

The Holy Spirit!

Time and again the Scriptures tell us of a Comforter, an Intercessor, a source of power available to us in the past and now. *Today.*

Though there are many books in the stores about the Holy Spirit and the Spirit-filled life, I hadn't been introduced to them then. However, the Bible, especially the book of Acts, is *full* of references to the Holy Spirit, a power I'd never thought of inviting into my life. I knew, of course, how Jesus had told His disciples to wait for the Holy Spirit to come to them and how at Pentecost they'd heard a noise like a rushing wind and received the Holy Spirit, and such power that they worked wonders. [1]

And a rough, cowardly fisherman named Peter became bold enough to witness—to serve—and to die!

Still, according to most authorities in the Church of Christ of which we were members, Pentecost was a first century thing after which the Holy Spirit—though He was still a part of the Trinity—had more or less rested on His laurels. According to predominant thinking in our church, He had inspired and established the Scriptures so that now no one needed "signs and wonders." [2]

Pat and I had been taught that the Holy Spirit's assignment had been to bring about the Bible in its finished form, and after that He'd been relieved of duty.

That, to me, didn't seem quite reasonable. To me, that view put the Holy Spirit in the category with a fine physician who expects to pass on all of his knowledge simply by writing an excellent, detailed textbook. Students could learn a lot of theory from reading such a book; but unless they went into a hospital and saw the doctor at work putting his theory into practice, they'd never fully appreciate all that he had to offer.

In other words, the student who knows the practice of medicine *only as theory* could hardly commit himself to it as completely as could the student who has seen it in operation and had *witnessed its effects*.

It's the result that confirms the theory! [3]

So the idea of a Holy Spirit in semiretirement, a source of divine theory but no longer transmitting divine power to Christians, was hard for me to accept. Therefore, relying upon the Scriptural promise that, if I knocked, the door would be opened, *I determined to learn more about the Holy Spirit*, the Comforter and Advocate whom Christ had promised "those who believe."

This was the first step in the greatest adventure of my life.

13
Language Of Love

I'm afraid most people consider speaking in tongues a weird, cultish practice of the ignorant, illiterate and hysterical.

So, often through our own ignorance, we condemn "tongues" as a substitution of emotion for intellect, and a pretty embarrassing one at that. And, I must confess, that's pretty much the way I used to feel. I'd never spoken out or lifted my arms in church, and the idea of anyone doing so made me uncomfortable.

If at the outset I'd realized what the Holy Spirit was going to lead me through, I might have said, "No thanks!" For, as I began my search for a personal encounter with the Spirit of God, a hunger to become "freakish" was certainly *not* a motivating factor.

At that time, while I'd never heard the phrase "baptism of, in or with the Holy Spirit" nor read *The Cross and the Switchblade* or any other book describing this great blessing, I had had one meeting with an industrialist named

George Otis who, I knew, was very close to God and incidentally had spoken in "unknown" tongues.

Pat, I knew, had the greatest respect for George as an intelligent man who was successful in the business world and in no way a hysterical misfit.

I'd met George and his wife, Virginia, when they'd come by our house to bring Pat some Bible tapes and had stayed to go with us to dinner and to a charity basketball game in which Pat was playing. That evening had been my one substantial contact with George until the morning he joined me and a friend of mine named Merlyn for breakfast.

Merlyn, too, had spoken in tongues and was having great trouble with his church because of it. I was sympathetic because I knew he truly loved God; but since I knew practically nothing about "tongues," I couldn't give him real guidance or encouragement. However, remembering that I'd just become acquainted with another man who spoke in tongues, it occurred to me that George Otis might be the very person Merlyn should talk with. So I invited the Otises to join Merlyn and me for breakfast at the Beverly Hills Hotel.

The Beverly Hills Hotel! A curious place indeed to be prepared for Pentecost. Yet the Lord is omniscient and omnipotent and can work in the Polo Lounge just as well as in a cathedral. Anyway, they shared their knowledge of the Holy Spirit with me, and, oh, how hungrily I received it. I was so hungry for more of the Lord that I seized on their every sentence like a starving person who's being offered bread. They were telling me about a Person—a Presence, a power, a reality—not a doctrinal belief. They *knew* this Person intimately and had daily fellowship with Him.

After breakfast, all of us came back to our house and, settling in the den, continued our talk. Finally George asked, "Shirley, have you ever asked Jesus to baptize you with the Holy Spirit?"

I said I guessed not—because I didn't know I was supposed to! I knew Merlyn had undergone something quite remarkable and quite valid. But I thought God had just "plopped" it on Merlyn, which was nice, but I hadn't known that I was supposed to enjoy anything similar (or even *could*).

George set me straight about that. Referring to many verses of Scripture, he showed me how the baptism of the Holy Spirit had been promised to all Christians, and how Jesus had told His disciples that they *needed* the power of the Holy Spirit in their lives before they could carry out their ministry.

That word *power* turned me on because what I needed at that instant was *power*—power to resist temptation, power to stand up for God—if I were going to be the kind of Christian I wanted to be. I'd always wanted to lead a good Christian life, but I'd failed most miserably. I'd been too weak to avoid the traps the devil had set, and I was afraid that, without extra strength, I'd succumb to them again.

So I said, "Wow! Power is what I need if I'm going to mean anything for Jesus and lead the life I'd like to lead."

What a disappointing witness I'd been in the past. But I prayerfully hoped, through the help of the Holy Spirit, that perhaps I could make the most of a second chance. I was thinking (though I couldn't say it), *I wish my company would leave so that I can be alone with the Lord,* when George, as though picking up my thought, told me, "Shirley, I believe we're supposed to leave—so that you can be alone with God."

Then they left!

But before going, George counseled me. He told me to confess to God *every sin I could remember,* and involvement in strange cults, any credence I'd placed in astrology, every error—even the most minute—I could bring to mind.

I'd never dabbled in any strange cult, but I had often read the horoscope column in the newspaper, so I added that to my list of transgressions and, a few minutes later in my room, was confessing to this along with everything else.

For several months, since the night at church when I'd recommitted my life to Christ, I'd been drawing closer to God. And now I was happily confident that He'd led George into my life because I was ready for a closer walk with the Lord. On my knees beside my bed I began earnestly to pray, couching my prayer in Scripture. I knew how easily the devil had fooled me before, leading me to rationalize and pretend that vice was virtue. And I wasn't going to be fooled again!

So I let the Bible lead me as I poured out my shortcomings to my heavenly Father. I confessed that by my bad example I'd damaged others connected with the entertainment industry. I named names and prayed that God would give me another chance to reach those I should have helped. I confessed my failures as a wife and mother. Every sin that I could bring to mind, I laid at Jesus feet.

When I'd confessed it all—I was filled with excitement and anticipation. I begged, "Lord, if there really is something extra available to a Christian, a power that comes through the Holy Spirit, please give it to me. I want everything You have to offer, whatever the cost in return. If tongues is part of this power, I'm willing. I just want *more of you!*"

Asking Jesus to cover all my many, many sins with His blood, I quoted the Scripture verse wherein He promised that, if I asked for bread, *I wouldn't be given a stone*; that, if I knocked, *the door would be opened.* [1] I said, "Lord, I'm asking to be filled with the Holy Spirit. I don't want more of Satan, so please, if this power is available to me, *please fill me with the Holy Spirit,* and I will give You my life, my voice, anything."

The room was so quiet—yet I didn't feel alone.

Remembering that in Acts 2 "they were all filled with the Holy Spirit and they began to speak with other tongues as the Spirit gave utterance," I deliberately began to utter little syllables, sounds, anything that seemed to want to come out of my mouth.

I wanted to tell Jesus how much I loved Him. I wanted to praise Him! At first I knew that the sounds came only from me. But suddenly—*rivers* of words poured forth, gushing, flowing cascades of sound, that sprang from so deep within me that I could feel their rush before they passed my lips! An overflow of a language I'd never learned was coming from me with such speed that I normally wouldn't have been able to think that fast even in English! But, strangely, though I didn't understand the words I was saying, *I understood my prayer.* Events in my life as far back as my childhood were covered in my plea that God accept and renew me.

As I prayed, I realized that *a great cleansing process* was taking place. And, while I was aware of that, I was even more aware of the presence of Jesus—pouring the Holy Spirit out upon me like warm oil, soothing, healing, restoring. At the same time I knew that He was telling me He loved me with a beautiful, perfect love, in such abundance that it filled and surrounded me.

Love was what I'd needed so badly and, receiving it, I was overjoyed. I'd longed for love, but because I'd been so unlovable I'd been sure that no one could give it—not acquaintances in the industry, not my children, not even my husband.

Because I knew I was thoroughly unworthy, the realization that God loved me *anyway* was so precious that I reached out my hands to Him. In a response I'd never made in any church, I instinctively lifted up my face and my hands in a gesture that—though I didn't know it—was completely scriptural.

Neither the Baptist Church nor the Church of Christ had taught me about "lifting up holy hands" to the Lord as in 1 Timothy 2:8. Yet the Bible often refers to the gesture.

Guided by the Holy Spirit within me, I raised my hands spontaneously in the way that a little child lifts up his when he runs to his daddy for help.

Our minister had pointed out that upraised hands are the international symbol of surrender; what could be more appropriate when you're completely surrendering to God? I'd never thought of that until he mentioned it; my action, as I knelt by my bed, was completely spontaneous.

By this time, I was crying. I was weeping great cleansing tears of *joy* because I'd been reassured that I was a child of the living God! Who in this whole world *wouldn't* burst with praise and devotion if the God of heaven and earth reached out to touch her intimately and individually? I knew His Spirit was bearing witness with mine that I was a child of God! [2] What unspeakable joy!

Eventually, I realized that *45 minutes* had been literally consumed with praise and adoration! Never before could I have *imagined* such a thing! And as silence returned, I was left with an "afterglow" of peace and well-being that is just indescribable.

Finally, as I rose from prayer, I strongly felt there were two people I should tell about what had happened to me: Pat and my sister, Julie.

Pat was out of town, but I called him at once.

"Wonderful, honey! Maybe it'll happen to me before long," he said.

However, I wasn't sure I should call Julie so quickly. Since she lives only a few miles from us, I thought, *I'll wait until we get together. I want to tell her about this in person, not over the phone.* So I waited. And I waited. And I waited.

As a matter of fact, six or eight weeks went by before Julie and I got together—and then it was to prepare for our daddy's funeral.

He died quite suddenly in Fort Wayne, Indiana, while Pat was away from home, so I received word of our loss without my husband's comforting presence.

We buried Daddy in 1968 on Debb's birthday and, as we arrived at the funeral parlor, I was afraid my heart would break, for I loved my father very much. However, his widow, Sally, was so completely torn up that I was more preoccupied with *her* grief than with my own. Sally was doing what I would have done a few weeks earlier—looking for an escape from the reality of our loss.

Sally had reacted to Daddy's death by plunging into sedation. But the truth kept seeping in. Now, just before funeral services were to begin, she was on her feet—but also on the verge of collapse.

I had a knot in my stomach and felt my tears ready to fall. However, I, who would have been an escape artist, too, a few weeks earlier, was relying on my newly found strength in the Lord to sustain me. God, I knew, could use even Daddy's death to His glory.

During the three days just before the funeral, my sisters, Jenny and Julie, and I had been praying that in some way our sorrow would be turned to glorify Jesus. I didn't know what God would do to bring this about, but I knew He *could* do something if He would.

Meanwhile, choking back my own tears and warring against the enemy, self-pity, I was (much to my surprise) literally ordering Sally, "Get that head up. Daddy wouldn't want this. He'd want God to be glorified." I could hardly believe I was taking such authority, because I wasn't naturally authoritarian. I'd always turned to Pat for my strength. But now he wasn't with me because, as a pallbearer, he was riding in another car.

My eyes *were* on Jesus and, regardless of the waves around me, I wasn't going to let them be drawn away, because I knew that if I lost my contact with the Lord I'd sink. That's true in any experience. It's only when we take our eyes off Jesus that we become lost.

When we reached the church I was still afraid I'd break

down if I walked through the door and heard the hymns Daddy had loved, so I suggested to my sisters, "Let's join hands and pray one more time." I was thinking, *We're at the Red Sea, Lord. Now what do we do?*

We prayed a very simple prayer asking God to lighten our burden. "Lord," I said, "You've promised that Your yoke is easy and Your burden is light, so *please take this burden from us,* and we'll give You all the glory."

As I said, "Amen" I *literally felt a healing presence* comforting me and lifting the weight of my grief! My heart, which had been aching and heavy, was filled with such peace that I said to Jenny and Julie, "He's *with us!*"

Sally and my sister, Betty, were experiencing a small measure of this relief, but I knew at once that Julie and Jenny were, because they were smiling. In that instant, God had become our Deliverer and Comforter. He'd taken over. I wasn't aware that photographers were taking our pictures as we went into the church, but later, when I saw the newspapers, I saw pictures of Sally, blank and numb with despair, and of me, Jenny and Julie, smiling!

Pat isn't an overly emotional person. However, during the service he cried. On the other hand, we Foleys, who usually cry even when we're happy—let alone when we're sad—were actually beaming with the peace of God. We *knew* that the body in the casket wasn't really Daddy, for he had gone on to eternal joy with the Lord.

At Daddy's funeral we together tapped a power that had become so real and intimate to me on that day when, on my knees in my room, I'd spoken in an unknown tongue.

Soon I would find it in action everywhere!

14

Am I Taking My Children To Hell?

In Nashville, the next day, Julie wanted to go to a Bible study at the home of a very dear friend of hers, and I asked her to let me tag along. My decision to go was a last-minute thing, but when I got there I was asked to share with the group some of my own religious views. To that point, I hadn't told Julie how I'd been baptized with the Holy Spirit, nor had I even heard such baptism defined.

However, I did feel impressed to describe to the women we were with the wonderful thing which had happened to me. Just as I began to speak, one woman jumped up, excused herself, and said she'd just remembered it was her day with her car pool. Out the door she shot, and I, somewhat relieved, believed I'd gotten a message from God. *He doesn't want me to say any more right now,* I thought.

Right after the woman left, another woman spoke.

"Shirley," she asked point blank, "have you received the Holy Spirit?"

Now what could I say to that? I told her I really didn't

know, that while something wonderful had occurred, I didn't know what to call it. Then I related my experience to the group, which was so beautifully receptive that since then each woman who was present then has received the Holy Spirit too!

This episode perfectly illustrated the beautiful timing of God; for Julie later confided that, had I spoken to her of my experience at any other place and with any other group, she might have thought I'd gone crazy.

Yet, with good friends whom she loved and trusted and who encouraged my disclosure, she was able to accept what I told her with an open mind. Soon Julie, too, received the Holy Spirit, leaving Jenny convinced for a time that she was the only "sane" member of the family! "Julie and Shirley have flipped," was her conclusion.

Eventually she began going with us to Bible classes, but for a long time she couldn't quite open up to all the blessings God wanted her to enjoy. She used her husband as an excuse. "Les would never accept this," she said.

But, after Les received the Holy Spirit, Jenny ran out of excuses and, at last, became joyously Spirit-filled too.

Jenny and her husband, Julie and hers, Pat, his secretaries, all the children—so many lives we've touched have been changed as the Holy Spirit has taken over.

I can understand why Jenny was slow to credit my experience, for even after Daddy's funeral, the Holy Spirit found *me* a doubting and shaky vessel for His power. I didn't understand His presence myself and went through one period of sheer torment during which I wondered whether the devil had taken charge of me after all.

As I've mentioned, the Church of Christ taught that the Holy Spirit had completed His work in Apostolic times, so the members I knew were not particularly cordial to my new experiences. One day, I mentioned to a minister friend the perfection of God's timing, for I'd received the baptism in the Holy Spirit in a period of repeated crises—just when I had an unusual *need* for His comfort and power.

Through death our family had lost three people very close to us in a period of only three months: my father, Pat's grandfather, and a dear friend of Cherry's. In addition we were burdened with severe financial problems which, at that point, seemed insoluble. It's at such critical times that you might blow your brains out unless you have something beyond yourself to uphold you. Therefore, I was particularly thankful that the Lord had so graciously sustained me through the power of the Comforter, and I said so.

The minister with whom I was sharing my thoughts looked at me wonderingly.

"Shirley," he said, "you really are becoming a *mystic,* aren't you?" Then, putting an arm around Lindy, he admonished her, "Don't let your mother make a nun out of you."

After that, all the way home in the car, I was silent, digesting his words and battling against the train of thought they'd started. His actual comment didn't bother me much, but his clear inference did: that I was on the wrong track, following guidelines which were dangerous, perhaps damning! And taking my children with me!

I'd found my new, happy relationship with God thrilling, but now I began to wonder, "Can my new beliefs harm my children? Am I going to lead them in a direction that might hurt them? Even cost them their souls?"

When my children are involved in anything, I walk softly. For *me* to err is one thing, but for me to lead *them* into error is quite another.

"Oh God," I prayed, "I hate to question these beautiful experiences, but now my children are involved—if my new language is from You, please let me know."

If God were trying to let me know, I couldn't hear Him, and that night I went to bed too miserable to rest.

"Honey," Pat demanded, "what's wrong? What's happened to you?"

He'd seen such a change for the good in me, such confidence since I received the Holy Spirit that he sensed instantly that something awful had happened.

"Nothing. I don't want to talk about it."

"Shirley, come on. Honey, something *is* bothering you. I know it. Now tell me what it is."

"I want to go to sleep," I said, not very truthfully, because I wasn't sure I could sleep at all. But I was back playing my old game, trying to escape from facing the issue.

Now Pat at this time hadn't received the Holy Spirit, but, just because of the change he'd seen in *me*, he knew my experience had come from God and not from the devil.

"You're not letting what was said tonight upset you, are you?" Pat demanded. "Forget it. He has no idea of what's happened to you!"

However, the devil, knowing my most vulnerable spot, was letting me have it where it hurt. If I wanted to go to hell, he whispered, that was my business—but how could I, through my error, endanger my girls?

Again and again, I silently begged God, "Please reassure me. Please give me a sign." And God, always faithful, did just that.

Just as I was dozing off, I began to pray subconsciously in my prayer language from which one phrase detached itself to lodge in my mind.

"Avidium, Avidium," I said, once, twice, over and over.

"Hey!" Pat was wide awake now. "Say that slower, please. Do you know what exactly you are saying? You're praising God in Latin! That's exactly what you're saying—*Ave Deum*—'Praise God!' *Now* do you believe your language comes from God? Do you think Satan would have you praise God in a language you don't even know?"

His reasoning was exciting and convincing, for I'd never studied Latin a day in my life, nor had I, so far as I could recall, ever heard the phrase!

It has been argued that I'd heard *Ave Deum* somewhere and dredged it up from my subconscious; but, even if this were the case, *its recall was still a miracle*. God had known my need and supplied it—whether from my subconscious or out of infinity.

Crying with relief, I asked Pat, "Would you kneel with me so that we can pray together? You've never heard me pray in my new language, but now I want you to."

So we knelt by our bed and, in a language I didn't understand, I began praising the Lord for His goodness. Pat said that, at that moment, he was more certain than ever the language was from God, for he felt a supreme love engulf us—love and peace and joy. Further, though he didn't know what I was saying either, he was convinced by my intonation and phrasing that I was speaking a genuine language, not just making unrelated noises.

By this time, you would think, I would have been sure beyond all questioning that my prayer language was a holy gift received from the Holy Spirit. But I remained aggravatingly human and, therefore, plagued by recurring doubts.

Suppose, I thought, *I said something that only sounded like "Ave Deum." Maybe I didn't say that at all.*

That's the way the devil baits us. In fact, he was after me from all directions, for I'd just heard an ugly rumor to the effect that I'd become an alcoholic and had been freed from my sickness by a mystic of some kind. That was false from start to finish. I hadn't become an alcoholic; though, who knows, I *might* have become one had I continued on my earlier, party-oriented path.

Trying to escape my confusion, I'd already asked God for a sign that my new language had come from Him. He gave me one which should have been enough for anybody, but, like doubting Thomas, I had to have *more* evidence.

"God," I pleaded, "hasn't anyone else in the Church of Christ ever had this experience? Please tell me someone else has." There's comfort in a crowd, you know!

Pat had to go out of town right away, so that next Sunday the girls and I were going to church alone. I was terrified that, because of my unorthodox beliefs, I was going to be called before the elders to answer for my alleged errors. So, just before I left the house for the service, I knelt to pray again.

Pat, my earthly strength, was gone, so I had to totally lean on the Lord. I prayed in the Spirit and, for a second time, a phrase isolated itself from my petition. Then another. "Te Amo Dominus." Then, "Deum amamas."

I couldn't forget the phrases, so as I drove toward church I asked Cherry, who was taking her second year of Latin, whether they meant anything to her.

"Sure," she said. "The first is, 'I love You, Lord,' and the second is, 'We love You, God.' Why? Where did you learn that?"

Being an emotional Foley, I almost had to pull off the freeway, for tears threatened to blind me.

(If you're a doubting Thomas and question this experience: Cherry is a straight A student and never needs my help. I have never seen a Latin book to my knowledge. You'll just have to accept that in faith!)

"Satan," I warned the devil, "you've lost this round. In the name of Jesus, you're not going to rob me of this blessing. So just don't try!"

The next morning I awakened with a great peace which has never left me. And that very day I received another concrete answer to prayer. A letter for me arrived from someone who'd seen an article I'd written in *The Twentieth Century Christian* about Daddy's death.

The stranger wrote: "I want you to know there are many of us in the Church of Christ on the West Coast who have also received the Holy Spirit."

Hallelujah! The Lord had reassured me. I wasn't alone in my church, after all.

And soon I wasn't alone in my family, either, for Pat and the girls were about to become Spirit-filled.

15
Getting Shirley Out Of The Way

The Bible tells us that nine "gifts" or abilities come through the Holy Spirit. Listed by Paul in 1 Corinthians 12, they are:

1. the "word of wisdom"
2. the "word of knowledge"
3. the gift of faith
4. the gifts of healing
5. the working of miracles
6. the gift of prophecy
7. the discerning of spirits
8. the gift of tongues
9. the interpretation of tongues

These gifts don't come with the baptism in the Holy Spirit because we deserve them or have earned them, but they are generously given expressions of God's love. And they're usually given only when God sees we need and are ready for them!

Dennis Bennett in his book, *The Holy Spirit and You,* compares gifts of the Spirit to the gifts a child receives from his parents on his birthday. The parents don't necessarily give presents because their child has been a model of perfect behavior, but because they love him, perfect or otherwise. And God's gifts are without repentance.[1] That is, once he gives the gifts, we either abuse them or use them for His glory.

I won't try to go into detailed, technical explanations of the spiritual gifts here for other books on this subject are available, written by persons who are much more expert than I.

I simply want to share how life in the Boone family has changed since Pat, the girls and I received the baptism in the Holy Spirit, and how gifts of the Spirit have helped us and others. As you read some of the following pages—the chapter on sex education, for example—you may shrug and think, "So? What's so spiritual about that? That's simply the Boones' opinion." Or, if you're more kindly disposed, you may say, "That's only common sense."

Other episodes may strike you as pure coincidence. But I believe that even the most cynical will have to accept that certain events I'm about to describe are *genuine miracles*, if you believe I'm writing the truth as I know it.

We Boones are beginners in our walk with the Holy Spirit. We're still asking questions. Probably we always will be. But we are growing and discovering, and everyday we reach a higher plateau. We're learning line upon line, precept upon precept, and we're going from glory to glory.

I believe that *every gift* offered by the Holy Spirit has operated in our lives at one time or another; however, we aren't too concerned about which gift is which or which is operating on one occasion or which on another, for the gifts come according to our need. God knows—and God gives![2]

For example, if someone were seriously ill, I wouldn't want the gift of prophesy so much as I'd want the gift of healing! So, while we may not always *define* the gifts precisely, we use each as it comes and, in Jesus' name, thank God for it.

Remember how Moses, standing before the burning bush, debated with the Lord who'd just told him to confront Pharaoh, pleading, "But, God, I can't."

And how God, showing divine patience in the face of Moses' obstinacy and lack of faith, said, "Follow My command, and I'll be with you. I will be *with thy mouth*, and will teach you what you shall do!"

Well, since my baptism in the Holy Spirit, I've discovered that God is not only with me, but He'll direct and counsel me if only I'll be quiet and listen.

"Be still, and know that I am God." [3] What a wonderful statement that is. How greatly each of us can profit from doing it.

As I've said, when I was baptized in the Holy Spirit, I not only didn't know what had happened; I didn't know what to *expect*.

But as days passed and I continued my prayer and study, my understanding increased. Thanks to the Holy Spirit, previously obscure passages of Scripture became clear. Further, when I took problems to God, His answers came back to my heart, usually indisputably distinct.

Because Pat had been for so long the spiritual leader in our home, it was uncomfortable at first to find our situation reversed. Because he was well grounded in the Scripture, he was quickly convinced that I'd experienced my own glorious Pentecost—and said he intended to experience the same wonderful baptism.

"I'll be right behind you," he promised.

Yet, for several months he wasn't.

Filled with the Spirit, I'd been introduced to a joy which, at that point, was unknown to Pat. And frankly, while I welcomed my new condition, I felt a little bit guilty about it.

It isn't my place to be Pat's spiritual leader, I thought. *He'd been mine before, and he should be mine now.* But, as things stood, my spiritual development was ahead of his, and there was nothing I could do about it. Nothing except pray. So, on my knees, I asked God for help.

I didn't want to be a spiritual teacher to Pat. For a wife to take such a dominant role just didn't seem proper. Only God could straighten things out.

I knelt, I prayed and I listened and, as I did, God spoke to my heart, so unmistakably.

"You're Pat's wife and helpmeet, aren't you?" God asked.

"Yes, Lord," I told Him.

"You're willing to wash his socks and care for his children and minister to his physical needs?"

"Oh, yes, Lord, I am."

"Then," God demanded, "why won't you be his spiritual helpmeet? Why are you so reluctant to accept that role?"

I'm afraid my jaw literally dropped at that.

Of course. The reasoning was so right and logical. Why should I, who was willing to darn Pat's socks and minister to him physically, hesitate to minister to him spiritually?

I saw that my attitude had been ridiculous. So from that time on, until Pat, too, was baptized in the Holy Spirit, I accepted—as a blessing—the responsibility of helping him spiritually. It was really more like sharing and supporting him until his full strength came.

Since Pat's been filled with the Holy Spirit, he's outstripped me in spiritual growth and understanding. He's been used by God in marvelous ways. He *is* head of our house, spiritually as well as in every other respect.

To return to the story of Moses, you remember how, as he was guided by the Lord, miracle upon miracle occurred. He left Egypt with almost two million men, women and children, acting upon God's promise that He would preserve them. And though the people doubted God's word, it was always good. The Red Sea parted, manna came, and water gushed from a rock in the dry desert.

Comparably, in the *New Testament*, Peter walked on water until he began to doubt. Buoyed by faith, he confidently approached Christ, until, as his belief was replaced by fear, the miracle ended.

I, too, have been buoyed by faith and participated in wonders since my Pentecost. My experiences weren't nearly as dramatic as Moses' or Peter's, but they demonstrate that if we aren't discouraged by our Red Sea, if we step boldly out of the boat, relying on Christ, our trust will be rewarded.

Until my baptism in the Spirit, I was shy. I would have no more made a speech in front of an audience than I would have tried to vault the Grand Canyon on a motorcycle! So one day when Prentice Meador, a friend of ours who teaches at UCLA, asked me to make a speech, I was initially dumbfounded.

He arrived unexpectedly at our door, announcing, "Shirley, I want you to talk to my communications class about your new spiritual experiences."

"Me?"

I stared blankly for an instant, trying to assimilate what he'd said.

"Why don't you ask Pat?"

"Because Pat won't be available at the time I'll need the speaker," he said.

"And when is that?"

"In ten minutes."

In ten minutes Prentice wanted shy me to make a talk *without preparation or notes* before a class of sophisticated UCLA students? I was instinctively shaking my head before I could find my voice.

But then I thought of the opportunity I was being given to share my Lord with young people. In the name of Jesus, I asked the Spirit's instruction. And, probably surprising

Prentice out of his wits, I said I'd be glad to speak to his class. And I was more surprised than *he* was!

I can't remember what I said, but I was cordially received. And at the end of the school term when Prentice asked the students which speaker they'd enjoyed most, the majority said, "Shirley Boone."

Now that, you'd better believe, was a little miracle!

The professor later sent me some of the complimentary statements the young people had written about my talk—a talk delivered with no preperation by a shy and inexperienced speaker—in answer to their exam question: to discuss the most impressive visitor and tell why. A typical statement read in part:

> Probably the most memorable guest in the class was Mrs. Shirley Boone. Her major strength came in not so much what she said (several of the other guests were as interesting in content) but in how she expressed herself. Her manner during her visit to the class was straightforward and direct, and she was extremely personal. The fact that she talked from her own feelings and experiences and wasn't afraid to bare her soul made her seem as though each of us had been personal friends. Her warm and open manner brought a sincerity that the other guests worked hard to obtain, and even those in the class who were skeptical about the existence of any charismatic powers (myself included) were awed by her presence and moved by the change she had so obviously experienced.

I appreciated the kind words but hope the student eventually realizes that it was a Presence other than mine which awed and moved him.

On another occasion, Pat was asked to attend a Baptist convention in Denver to show film from his picture, *The Cross and the Switchblade*. The invitation came at a time when Pat was away from home and wouldn't have time to get back to Los Angeles, pick up the film, and return to Denver before his scheduled convention appearance. So he asked me to bring it to him in Colorado.

I did, and was sitting with him on the platform in the center of 14,000 people, Baptist ministers and wives, when time came for his presentation.

As things turned out, something was wrong with the projection equipment, so Pat couldn't screen the film footage but, never at a loss for words, he carried on.

"They asked me to show you the film—so here it is," he said, holding up a can of film. Then he explained why the picture couldn't be screened, and made this comparison: "Our Christianity is too often like this can of film. It may be real, but *unless it's seen in action and living color,* it won't mean anything to others."

Then he concluded by introducing me.

"My wife, Shirley," Pat finished, "who would also like to say something."

Oh, no, I wouldn't!

At least I was sure I had nothing to say—until I found myself on my feet speaking. As I talked, I moved around the platform to face each section of the audience, until, suddenly realizing I'd completed my thought, I found myself back where I'd started, beside Pat.

Again, I was not sure what I said, but as I sat down, the audience gave me a standing ovation.

If I'd tried to time my remarks to tally with my turn around the platform, the timing couldn't have been more perfect. All that I did was instinctive. All that I said was spontaneous. It wasn't I but the Holy Spirit who had been in charge, giving me the words and timing I needed to glorify Jesus.

When you need the right word to tell another about Christ, pray—and the word will be provided. When you need guidance—a sign to point you in the right direction—pray. If you pray with faith, God will answer.

Sometimes, I'll admit, it's a little tricky figuring out just what His answer means. But, if you'll continue to pray, asking the Spirit to guide you for the glory of Christ, you'll get your direction. And even if you misunderstand and make the wrong turn, the Lord will turn your mistakes around and use *them* for your good. [4]

Since the Scripture warns us that *we don't know our own hearts*. [5] it's urgently important that we stay closely tuned in to the Holy Spirit. Otherwise, in the way that a radio signal can be blocked by lead, "self" can block impulses from God.

How often when you pray for this or that can you be sure of your motivation? Entirely too often I have to admit in prayer that I don't know my heart and don't entirely trust it. It's then that I ask God, "Please rid me of 'self' and use me to Your glory. You, Lord, know my heart; if my motives are selfish, cleanse me of them."

In moments of prayer such as these, I fall back on the gifts of the Spirit: knowledge, wisdom, faith.

Before Pat wrote *A New Song*, we agonized a long time over our motives and over the wisdom of sharing so much of our most personal lives with the public. A number of people have been suspicious of Pat's reason for writing his confession, but we didn't turn the manuscript over to the publisher until we'd prayed long and earnestly and were *sure* that our motivation was Christ-centered—not self-centered.

We would have torn up the book after the last chapter was written had we not believed that God approved it. The Lord graciously gave us sign after sign to let us know He was blessing the writing and would bless the book's use.

In the same way, I agreed with some trepidation to write *this* book. I felt terribly inadequate to write a book. And I wondered who would care about what I had to say. I expect some readers may question my motivation, too.

However, because of what the Father, Son and Holy

Spirit have done for me, I have a story I can't contain. So, I'm offering my "fish and loaves" and asking the Lord to bless it and feed some of His hungry multitudes.

If you'll think back to the first time you fell in love, you'll remember how you wanted to shout your joy from the housetops. Well, the love which surrounds me now is so great, I want to shout about it too!

Thus the book.

Gertrude Stein wrote, "A rose is a rose is a rose."

And the same goes for miracles.

A miracle is a miracle is a miracle.

The fact that I could make a successful, impromptu speech at UCLA was miracle enough to convince me that, with God the Holy Spirit, all things are possible.

But, if you'd like *more* evidence, in the next chapter I'll tell you about a miracle which gave an agnostic engineer— who'd said he only believed what he could feel, see and touch—the jolt of his life.

And I'll also tell you about a woman who was seeking God's help with a very serious problem: terminal cancer!

16
Miracles Of Millie And The Mouse

"A miracle is a miracle is a miracle," Gertrude Stein might have written if she had been a believer.

God's miracles, large and small, are equal in importance, because each glorifies Him. However, when viewed from a human perspective, miracles vary in significance. We see some as fortunate little happenings which might be written off as coincidences, while others are real mind-blowers!

Since my family has been filled with the Holy Spirit, we've witnessed or experienced *almost daily miracles* which make our lives increasingly exciting. For the Holy Spirit carrying out the will of God is a perpetual source of thrilling surprises. Jesus told Nicodemus that very thing. [1]

Well, some of the miracles we've encountered have been more stunning to the human mind than others. For example, the "Miracle of the Mouse" was less than was the "Miracle of the Repaired Punch Point." That one was a corker! Yet the two shouldn't be compared; for each was an act of God, serving His divine purpose.

Let me tell you about both miracles—and you'll see what I mean.

The mouse which may have, through its history, saved more souls than some preachers, had been a preChristmas gift to Lindy from one of her friends. Because Debby had a pet mouse, Lindy had asked for one for Christmas, planning to breed her pet with her sister's and raise baby mice for pet stores. I think the girls had heard that stores would pay fifty or seventy-five cents each for the babies, so they had visions of becoming "mouse moguls."

Lindy, assuming that Pat and I weren't keen about giving her a mouse for Christmas, had mentioned her longing to her closest friend. So it just happened that a few days before Christmas, Lindy had become the pleased owner of a little brown and white mouse.

Shortly afterward, while I was out shopping with Cherry and Debby, Pat was in the den talking with Tom Harris, associate producer of *The Cross and the Switchblade*, when Lindy came in with cupped hands and tear-filled eyes.

Realizing at once that something was terribly wrong, Pat asked her, "What's the matter, honey?"

"Daddy," Lindy said, "can you take my little mouse to the vet right away?"

The idea of taking a mouse to a veterinarian was so incongruous Pat almost laughed. But, looking at Lindy, he knew that the situation wasn't at all funny to her. In fact, it was tragic, so he kept a straight face.

The mouse, curled in her cupped hands, looked dead, so Pat excused himself and called the pet store to get some advice. He described the mouse's condition to the store owner and asked, "Should we take it to a vet?"

The store owner laughed and said not to bother. A sick mouse, he said, was a dead mouse, and the best thing Pat could do with Lindy's pet would be to throw it away and get her another one.

"But I can't do that," Pat told him, "because Lindy has actually gotten attached to *this* one. Isn't there *anything* we can do? Can we give the mouse medicine?"

The pet store owner insisted that, so far as he knew, nothing could be done for an ailing mouse.

"A sick mouse is a dead mouse," he repeated. "You haven't had that one long, so I'll take responsibility for its condition. Let me give you a new one."

Pat was tempted to accept the offer; but looking at Lindy's face, he couldn't.

Our spiritual growth was in a very early stage then. But already, we had come to believe that God really was concerned with our specific daily problems, the most intimate ones, and that we should *take everything to Him in prayer.* So, remembering this, Pat suggested, "Lindy, let's go upstairs."

Then he, Lindy and Laury went upstairs with the mouse.

On the way, though, Pat's faith began to falter. Faith and mortal logic were warring.

"Wait a minute," Pat's logic said. "What if the Lord doesn't answer my prayer? What if the mouse dies *while we're praying for it?* What will that do to Lindy's faith? If God doesn't take any interest in this mouse, it won't bother me. But how will *Lindy* react? She's so emotionally involved."

Pat was concerned. Still, since he, the girls and the mouse by this time were upstairs in our bedroom where we've done so much of our praying, he said, "Let's pray about this."

So, as Lindy held the mouse, they knelt down together. First Pat read from the Bible the passage in which Jesus promised that if we ask with enough faith, we can move mountains. [2] Then he began to pray something like this:

"Lord, we're not asking that a mountain be cast into the sea. This morning we're just asking that this little mouse recover.

"You made this little mouse, so You must care about it, just as You care about Lindy and Laury and me. We care about the mouse, but we can't do anything for it. The vet can't and the pet store man can't. In fact, we know that *You're the only one* who can help this mouse, and, since we know You're concerned about every one of Your creatures and since Jesus promised that we might ask *anything* in His name, we believe that You will answer our prayer and help the little mouse.

"Lord, I've just read how Jesus thanked You *before* He called Lazarus out of the tomb. So I'm thanking You now for hearing us."

Just as Pat gave God his thanks, the mouse twitched in Lindy's cupped palms in what might have been a death agony. She didn't look at it but laid it on the bed and then, weeping, folded her hands.

Meanwhile, as Pat thanked God for helping the mouse, he felt his own faith increase and strengthen. He told me later that, as he thanked God for loving us, for allowing us to approach His throne with our most trivial concerns, for being a part of our lives, he and the girls were filled with confidence that the Lord was not only listening—but was granting their petition.

By this time, Pat and Laury, as well as Lindy, were crying, but they were shedding tears of joy instead of sorrow, because of their conviction that the Lord truly cared.

Finally they opened their eyes and raised their heads— and before them on the bed they saw the little mouse *sitting up wiping his nose with his front paws!*

He was still weak, but he was definitely alive and *much stronger* than he'd been a few minutes before! Lindy rushed to bring him some seed which he was too feeble to crack. However, he tried to crack it and, when he couldn't, he raked it underneath himself for safekeeping. In other words, he was planning for the future!

Next Lindy brought him some water—which he drank— and some lettuce, which he nibbled. Strengthened by the water and lettuce, he tried the seeds again, and this time he could crack and eat them.

While Pat and the girls watched, that mouse revived! I mean before their eyes—and within a half hour, he was friskier than he'd ever been. You can just imagine the joy of that scene in our bedroom; but unexpectedly Lindy began to cry again. To sob.

"What's the matter now?" Pat wanted to know.

"Daddy," Lindy told him, "there's more to this than you know."

Then she explained that in recent days she'd been talking with a boy who was older than she and quite intelligent, and who not only didn't share her faith but "put it down."

Using what had seemed to be almost irrefutable logic, he'd attacked her trust in God until Lindy, despite her desire to believe, had begun to doubt more than just a little. While the boy hadn't actually killed her faith, he had certainly stifled her fervor.

Lindy has an extremely logical mind, so she'd been highly susceptible to his arguments. Happily, she hadn't wrestled with her doubt alone but had eventually talked directly to God about it.

"Lord, I'm so confused!" she'd prayed. "Please do something totally illogical to strengthen my faith. Please show me that You do exist and are listening to me and that this boy is wrong."

When Pat and the girls had gone upstairs to pray for the mouse, Pat, though he didn't know then about Lindy's quandary, had worried for fear God would say "no" and Lindy's faith would be weakened. However, after we heard her full story, we were sure that the Lord had used her mouse to answer her earlier prayer. Lindy had asked God to restore and strengthen her belief in Him.

Sometimes God may test our faith, but if we trust Him, He's not going to let it be shattered. [3]

A friend of ours is a veterinarian, and when we told him what had happened, he said, "That *was* a miracle, because the pet store owner was right. *A sick mouse is a dead mouse!*"

I've said that this mouse has probably helped save more souls than some preachers, because after Pat told the story publicly, it spread—and has affected the thinking of numbers of people. Most surprisingly, he's seen "tough" businessmen wiping tears away upon hearing the Miracle of the Mouse.

I know that despite the vet's opinion, the mouse's recovery might be written off by an unbeliever as a coincidence. But *we know better*!

You would too if you could have seen the tears in Lindy's eyes, have been on your knees in that bedroom—and felt the ache in her young heart to *know* that God was listening to her. He was!

Now, two of the many other miracles we've encountered were so remarkable that even the most skeptical have found them impressive evidence that there is a power mightier than man.

I've always known that God has infinite power, but earlier in my life I'd seldom reached out for it because I'd been taught *that it wasn't available to me.* Now, though, since my family and I have been filled with the Holy Spirit, we realize that God's promises are ours to claim, so, when we pray, we aren't shy about saying, "Lord, please use us to bring glory to Your name."

Even so, when Pat was first asked to pray with Millie—he was reluctant.

Pat was appearing in Las Vegas when the minister of a church he attends there approached him about Millie. She was in a local hospital, he said, with *terminal cancer of the bone.* As a matter of fact, he continued, her bones were so riddled by cancer that she couldn't be turned in her bed for fear they would crumble. And she was in excruciating pain.

The sufferer was Catholic, the minister said, but after reading Pat's book, *A New Song*, she felt that if he'd come and pray with her, she'd be healed

146

Well, you can imagine how Pat felt about this.

He knew that *God* could cure Millie, but he wasn't sure that he, Pat Boone, was the proper mediator. He certainly couldn't visit the hospital in the role of faith healer or miracle worker, for he knew only God could perform miracles. So Pat hesitated. But after much prayer he realized that he *must* go. How could he say "no" to the dying woman's request?

There's a possibility, he thought, *that God has something wonderful in the works and is giving me an opportunity to share in it.*

So, a few days later, after calling the hospital first, he went to see Millie, who, it turned out, was the mother of the hospital administrator.

Every inch of the way to the hospital, Pat prayed, "Lord, if You are going to do something, please make it positive because I'm going out here in fear and trembling. I know I can't do anything for this lady. Here it is broad daylight, and in an hour I'm supposed to play golf with Perry Como. I'm just another flesh-and-blood guy, a creature of the plain old human world.

"Lord, I'm going out to see a lady I've never met who is expecting a miracle. Well, if something's going to happen, You'll have to do it, because *I* sure can't."

Then he went in to see Millie, who turned out to be a sweet little woman whose company he genuinely enjoyed. They talked some about Pat's book and about what the Lord had done in their lives. Finally Pat said, proving he definitely was of the human world, "I'm going to play golf with Perry Como."

Millie was delighted to hear that.

"Oh," she said, "I'm one of his biggest fans. Please tell him hello for me. I used to play golf myself until this happened. I played all the time. I even have my own golf cart."

Pat told her that maybe Perry would come out to see her.

However, she wanted something more than that.

"Before you go," she said, "let's pray. I wish you'd pray with me. Sit down here on the edge of the bed."

Because of her condition, Pat was afraid to sit on the bed. But she insisted, so he gingerly eased down by her side and took her hand and prayed. He didn't pray that God would heal her, but rather he said:

"Lord, I believe that Your hand is in this situation, and I know you love Millie and me. I believe that You are a God of miracles—so will You perform Your most perfect will for Millie? Please do the thing that You most want to do with her life and body, and we'll thank and praise You for it. In Jesus' name, Amen."

When Pat looked at Millie, she was crying.

"You just *talk* to God, don't you?" she asked.

"Well, sure," Pat said. "Don't you?"

"No," Millie told him, "I just say the prayers I learned as a Catholic."

"Well," Pat suggested, "after this why don't you try just talking with God? He's right here in the room, and He loves you more than anybody in this world loves you. So just talk with Him the way you talk with me."

Millie said that she would, and Pat promised that he'd come back to see her.

Later, playing golf with Perry and his wife, Pat told them about Millie, adding, "I believe God has something up His sleeve for her."

The next time Pat went to the hospital, nurses greeted him by saying that Millie's spirits were high and that his previous visit had done her a lot of good.

Pat and Millie prayed together again. Now Pat was actually looking forward to his talks with Millie because, despite her illness, she was so happy.

The third time Pat visited her, she said, "I want to be baptized with the Holy Spirit."

"Millie," Pat assured her, "it's as simple as just asking the Lord. It's between you and Him, for He's the Baptizer. I don't think I should necessarily be involved in it. When you're ready, just ask Him—He'll baptize you."

Pat didn't see Millie again during that visit to Vegas, but he wrote to her and kept praying for her. At first she wrote back, too, quite optimistically, about how they'd play golf the next time he was in town.

After a while, though, Pat's letters to Millie grew further apart, and she didn't write to him. Finally, his own wavering faith made him *afraid* to write!

In fact, when all of us went back to Las Vegas the following summer, he was afraid to call the hospital because of the news he might receive.

We were appearing at the Fremont Hotel, and one night, after the first show, the phone rang backstage. The call was for Pat.

"Pat Boone?" the caller said. "This is Millie. Do you remember me?"

Remember her? Pat almost shouted with joy!

"Of *course* I do, Millie," he said. "Where are you?"

"I'm in the lobby," she told him. "I just saw your show."

"Stay right where you are," Pat said. "We'll be with you in a minute." He grabbed my hand and we fairly flew out front!

In the lobby we found Millie with three nuns, one of whom was celebrating her sixtieth anniversary as a maid-servant of the Lord. The nuns called Millie their "little miracle."

And sure enough, she was! Her eyes were shining and her physical appearance and energy were living proof of God's miracle power.

"You know," Millie told Pat, "I just missed you in Chicago. I flew back to see some relatives there at the time that you and your family were giving a concert in Chicago. I didn't see it because it was sold out. And you'd left the next day when I tried to contact you."

The next week, Millie added, she was going to San Francisco to see her doctor for a checkup. She was going to see him, then she was going to see the Giants play ball. She was a real sports fan.

One of the nuns told me privately that, while Millie's bones still showed the *effects* of cancer, they were no longer deteriorating, *but had hardened,* and the ravages left by the disease didn't bother her at all!

Isn't God wonderful?

Because of Millie, this hospital has become something of a combination hospital and Bible school! And not only precious Millie received her baptism of the Holy Spirit; through her miracle and her joy, so have many others, including her dear sister nuns. The happy shock waves continue to radiate outward in ever widening circles from this dear little lady.

So—take your pick—Millie or the mouse. God blessed them both, and for His glory. They both demonstrate His wondrous love and His intimate concern.

We call them—miracles.

17
What's The Point Of Miracles?

Naturally people ask, "Why are some prayers answered while others aren't? Why does God perform one miracle and not another?"

I've asked those questions myself many times—and still do. Because of the miracle of the mouse, the faith of Lindy and her friends was not only renewed, it was made fervent; for they've seen that *God is real and accessible to everybody,*—and that He's interested in our most "trivial" problems.

The miracle of Millie has launched such a spreading of faith that its limits are unforeseeable. Through Millie, through the nuns, through doctors and other hospital personnel, the dramatic reminder that there *is* a God who loves us has gone to countless people.

Unfortunately *we too often place limits on God* through our lack of faith or through our unwillingness even to *ask* Him for something for fear He won't give it to us. Instead of confidently asking for miracles, we're too prone to speculate, "Suppose I ask God for such and such and He doesn't give it to me. I'll look pretty silly, won't I?"

Pat and I have been involved in a number of situations through which we exposed ourselves to ridicule if God didn't answer our prayers. But, at those times, we've remembered how Peter walked on water *until he began to doubt*. How the other disciples would have laughed if, when Peter got out of the boat, he'd sunk and come up sputtering!

Yet, even when we pray with what we believe is pure faith, things don't always work out according to our petitions. Through hindsight, I've discovered the reason for that. It's simply this: *God knows things we don't know.*

So now, when He doesn't answer a prayer the way I hoped He would, I tell Him, "OK, Lord, I realize that You know something about this that I don't understand. If I've been wrong, teach me. And, if You're dealing with something I'm not aware of, then praise Your name anyway."

When prayers aren't answered according to our petitions, I believe one of two things is responsible: Either we don't understand the situation and thus can't see that God is doing a greater work than we'd dreamed of—or that we haven't reconciled ourselves to God.

Admittedly it's not always easy to find God's perfect will. For example, members of a certain religious group handle poisonous snakes because they believe (rightly) that God can protect them from the venom. But is it God's will that they do this?

I know that God can protect them from the venom, but I wouldn't deliberately handle a poisonous snake simply to test the Lord. I feel that I'd be doing what Satan asked Jesus to do when he tempted Him to jump off a mountain. And as I remember, Jesus didn't jump!

Nor does my family rely totally on prayer when one of us is seriously ill. We do all that we can to help ourselves— which includes seeing a doctor sometimes, and after that we leave the cure to the Lord. We know that God gives us our wonderful doctors; but where their abilities cease—God's begin!

The whole purpose in our being here is to worship God, to have fellowship with Him and one another—and *to glorify Him.* Even in times of trial we should praise God, because hard times as well as happy ones are given us *for a purpose.* I believe with all my heart that all things work together for your good if you love the Lord.

That's why I rejoice now when I'm tried, for I'm sure that through those trials God is teaching me something and leading me to higher ground.

I've wondered what it means to be baptized with the Holy Spirit and *fire.* In Romans 5:3-6 we read that we should *glory in our tribulations,* because they work patience, experience and hope in us, and this causes the love of God to be "shed abroad in our hearts by the Holy Spirit." The Lord is purifying us with fire: testing, trails, tribulations—making us fine silver and gold.

Do you know how a professional silversmith refines silver? He takes it in its natural form, places it in fire, and keeps it there till the impurities surface, and then he scrapes off the dross. He watches it closely and doesn't allow the fire to get too hot because that would destroy the silver. The silversmith knows exactly when to remove the silver from the fire in its purest form—because he can see his image reflected in it!

With this understanding I rejoice in the Lord *always* [1], and I can give thanks always for *all things.* [2]

Praise God, through the fire, Christ is being formed in me. He leaves us in our tests, our trials, our tribulations until He can *see His image in us.* But we have his promise that He'll never allow us to undergo more than we can bear.

Paul, in his letter to the Corinthians, said, "I glory in my infirmities," so we know that he experienced human suffering. In fact, he had what seemed to be more than his share, and God didn't take his burdens from him. Instead, the Lord showed Paul that his troubles were blessings, allowed by His Father for a good purpose.

I believe that when the Lord acts, it's for a reason. He performs miracles not just for the sake of the miracles themselves, but to bring doubters to the truth, to show His grace and mercy, and to bring glory to His name.

The miracle of the punch point is a perfect illustration of God using His power for glorious purposes.

We have a Spirit-filled friend who works in the aerospace program with an agnostic engineer named Joel. Although Joel had been reared in a church, through his scientific education he had come to question the very existence of God and certainly the divinity of Christ.

Our friend, whom I'll call Ed, tried at lunch times to discuss Jesus with Joel, but he got such a cool, disinterested reception that finally he decided, "I'll wait for God to tell me when to speak. When He wants me to say more to Joel, He'll let me know."

He thought after this that he might never mention the subject to his co-worker again. But, to his surprise, once he'd turned the matter over to God, opportunities for discussions came as thick and fast, always instigated by Joel himself!

Still the talks didn't bring any concrete results. When Ed urged Joel to read the Bible, Joel answered that there'd be no point in it because he never had gotten anything out of his parents' Bible—the King James Version.

"No matter," Ed said. "I just happen to have a modern version which I'll be happy to lend you."

Then Joel's typical excuse was that he didn't have time just then for reading.

Shortly after this, Joel was assigned to work on a bearing container for a space vehicle. To carry out his task he personally designed and made a small punch similar in shape to a tiny automatic pencil. (The fact that Joel had himself designed and machined this piece of equipment was important to what happened next.)

Because Joel had more work to do than he could conveniently handle, Ed volunteered to work on the bearing container, using the punch Joel had designed and made. He was doing the work all alone in a sterile lab where there was no traffic, since only critical personnel were allowed in the area to prevent contamination.

Using the punch Joel had designed, Ed was working on the diminutive bearings when the point of the punch broke. Looking through a microscope, he could clearly see it still sticking into a bearing. He tried to remove it with pinchers, without success.

Next Ed tried working with the broken punch. Though the damaged instrument worked fairly well, the broken point left ragged marks on the bearings. Finally Ed laid the punch aside, concluding that he'd have to have another made in the company machine shop the next day.

Meanwhile he was thinking of Joel, his agnostic friend who'd said that he could only believe what he could see or touch. Opening his desk drawer, Ed saw a copy of Dennis Bennett's book, *The Holy Spirit and You,* which he'd brought in a few days before. Opening it casually, he found that he'd turned to a chapter on miracles! *"God expects to do miracles,"* he read, *"so Christians should never feel hesitant about asking for them."*

Ed didn't specifically pray just then that God would work any particular wonder to impress his friend. However, he prayed as he'd thought before, "Lord, if Joel is to believe, You're going to have to show him what You can do."

Ed turned to pick up the punch again, wondering whether it could still be used in some way. But, when he looked at it, his hair almost stood on end.

"I was afraid to touch it," he said later.

For the punch, which had been broken, was not only

repaired—*but had the brightest, most perfectly machined point Ed had ever seen.*

At last he picked it up and examined it. The "workmanship" was superb!

Using a microscope, he looked for the old broken point. There it was, still imbedded in a bearing.

"Joel," Ed finally called, "you've got to see this."

When Joel came in and saw the punch, he was surprised. "How did you get the new point on?" he demanded.

Ed didn't tell him at first but, instead, asked him to look through the microscope at the bearings.

"What do you see?"

"Well," Joel said, "it looks like a broken point is sticking into a bearing."

"That's right. Now tell me what else you see."

"Looking at the next two or three bearings, I see marks on them which seem to have been made with a broken punch."

"That's right."

"OK. But in that case, how did you get the new point on the punch?"

When Ed told Joel what happened, his friend walked out of the lab shaking his head. He had a miracle he could see and touch but couldn't instantly digest.

A minute or so later, though, he *came* back in, confessing, "It *had* to happen the way you said—because nothing else is *possible.*"

Then, after a second's pause, he added, "If you still have that Bible, I'd like to read it."

At present, he's still reading it, and how it's affecting his thinking he hasn't said. But his fine mind has been opened by an act of the Lord to the possibility that God loves him, that Jesus died for him, and that the Holy Spirit is ready to fill him with power.

I believe that God performed the miracle of the broken punch for the specific sake of this one man, for the reclaiming of this one straying soul.

I also believe, though, that if our friend Ed had asked God to machine a new point for the punch as a kind of magic trick, just to see whether He could do it, God would have been displeased.

I personally benefited from a healing miracle which God performed out of mercy and love.

On a morning when Pat, the girls and I were scheduled to fly to Nashville to share the Lord with a home Bible study group, I awoke with a severe attack of stomach flu. Feverish, aching, nauseated, I forced myself to get onto the plane because it was imperative that I make the trip.

When we arrived in Nashville, though, I was still so sick I could hardly raise my head from a pillow. I knew medicine wouldn't have me well in a few hours, so I didn't call a doctor. It seemed the flu would have to run its course.

But Pat's parents called a minister and some friends, all of whom had received the baptism of the Spirit, and asked if they might pray over me, lay hands on me, and anoint me with oil in the name of Jesus.

Since I knew this healing practice was biblical [3] though I'd never seen it applied, I welcomed their prayers. So, praising God quietly, prayerfully, they laid hands on me and the minister anointed me. At once I felt my illness go!

Well, I thought, *I feel so much better I'll go to sleep now, and when I wake up I'll be as good as new.*

But, amazingly, as weak as I had been, I didn't drift into sleep. Instead, I was suddenly filled with a sense of such well-being that I got out of bed at once, freed from every symptom of the flu.

In answer to prayer, the Lord had made me well— miraculously, because He loves me. I can't help but be deeply moved when I read in the Bible where Jesus did things like this over and over, to show us what God is like! [4]

God works miracles to show His mercy and love, to

redeem the lost, and to bring glory to Himself. He answers our prayers to show His love—not to satisfy our instant whims.

I found a poem, "Answered Prayer," which beautifully summarizes the graciousness of God. Because it explains so much, so well, and much better than I can, I'll let it speak for me here:

I asked for strength that I might achieve;
He made me weak that I might obey.
I asked for health that I might do greater things;
I was given grace that I might do better things.
I asked for riches that I might be happy;
I was given poverty that I might be wise.
I asked for power that I might have the praise of men;
I was given weakness that I might feel the need of God.
I asked for all things that I might enjoy life;
I was given life that I might enjoy all things.
I received nothing that I asked for,
All that I hoped for.
My prayer was answered!

author unknown

We may not always, instantly, perceive that God has heard our prayers. 5

Yet, by taking every problem to Him, every fear, and—yes—even our every doubt, as Lindy did, we can claim a miraculous bounty of happiness.

18
New Life In Hollywood

For a town that doesn't exist, Hollywood has a lot in common with other towns its size.

I say that Hollywood doesn't exist, because technically there's no such place. It has no city charter, no municipal boundaries, no mayor nor any corporate identity. Some people maintain that it's only a state of mind. Nothing more.

Yet Hollywood does have a population—unofficial though it may be—made up of all the people in the Los Angeles area who are associated with show business. Psychologically, it's their home, and among them you find all the fears, foibles, fantasies and frustrations found within the population of any other community.

Like other towns, Hollywood has births, deaths, and marriages. It has love affairs and unemployment and traffic snarls; in short, all the stuff from which life in general is made. However, in Hollywood, everything is intensified. Temptations are more tempting; ambition, more burning. Charm is more irresistible, and the beautiful people are superbly so and intensely conscious of the fact.

They'd better be.

They'd better be beautiful and know it if they're going to hang on in Hollywood.

There's a great potential for heartbreak among the gifted and gorgeous people of show business, for they live with its ingredients: the ambition and the temptation, not to mention the character-eroding flattery to which they're constantly subjected.

Yet there's also a great potential for triumph.

For, when the life of a beautiful and charismatic person becomes dedicated to Jesus, the scope of its influence can be beyond measure.

God can use the most humble "ordinary" person to His great glory, but how *greatly* He can use those He's endowed with exceptional magnetism—when it's invested for His sake.

Johnny Cash, to cite an example, has just recently been filled with the Holy Spirit, as has his wife, June, and soon after, as he completed a concert in Holland, he felt so strongly moved by the Lord that he gave an "altar call!"

In other words, at the end of his concert performance, Johnny, surprising himself perhaps as much as his audience, but sensing their spiritual hunger, extended God's great invitation.

Like a tent-meeting evangelist, he urged his listeners to come forward and accept salvation through Christ. And, in that foreign city, from among those who'd come to find entertainment rather than Jesus, an estimated *2,000 people responded!* Johnny was stunned. He'd never given an altar call before, and he certainly hadn't intended to give one as his concert "encore."

Yet, because he'd previously asked Christ to take charge of his life, the Lord had used him gloriously.

Since Pat and I were saved from Hollywood heartbreak only through surrender to God and baptism with the Holy Spirit, we empathize completely with others in the entertainment business who still have the same kind of snarled-up lives. Therefore, since Pat's book, *A New Song*, sums up our formula for happiness, we give copies to friends in the industry who may find it helpful or at least interesting. Please understand, our gift of a book is never intended as a "holier-than-thou" gesture. By sharing our story, we simply try to say to our friends that whatever their problems may be, ours have probably been worse—but that, through the Holy Spirit, we've experienced miracles.

And guess what? Entertainers are human beings, with souls and spiritual vacuums—like everybody else! For after receiving *their first knowledge* of God's offered Gift through *A New Song,* several Hollywood celebrities have sought the Holy Spirit and have received Him!

Most of these won't be identified here because their experiences with Jesus are personal and private matters which they, not I, should make public when the Lord leads them to do so.

However, with their permission, I want to tell the story of Jim and Carole Hampton, our friends of long standing, whose lives had been revolutionized as completely as Pat's and mine have been.

We've known Jim since before Cherry was born, when he and Pat attended North Texas State College together. Later, when Pat's work took him overseas, Jim was in the service stationed in Europe, and we saw him in Austria.

Later still, he worked for a syndicated news service, and at first one place and then another we encountered him taking pictures. In other words, our lives kept criss-crossing.

Jim is a natural comedian, a man gifted with a great sense of humor, so it wasn't surprising that he finally landed in Hollywood where he lived with us for a while. He's starred as the bugler in "F Troop," LeRoy in "The Doris Day Show" and other major TV shows and plays.

He, Pat and I had a lovely, warm relationship, enhanced when Pat introduced Jim to Carole, a talented singer-actress whom he soon married.

At first, after their marriage, the Hamptons visited us often, and the four of us indulged together in the phony, so-called fun which we thought then meant that we "belonged."

But, after I received the baptism of the Holy Spirit, Jim and Carole visited us less often. Pat and I were beginning sound a little "fanatical" to them, so they stayed away.

Then Pat was filled with the Spirit, and I suspect the Hamptons were genuinely alarmed. For they heard from various mutual friends crazy stories about us. They heard, for example, that we'd "started our own church," though actually we were in the same church that has existed since it was established by the Lord.

The rumors, which were disturbing Jim and Carole, got back to us—and we just laughed! It didn't bother us much what others said. Once we had cared deeply, but, filled with the Holy Spirit, we were on such a firm foundation that cruel gossip couldn't rattle us for long.

We didn't see Jim and Carole for a long time, but this was to be expected, because we didn't have much in common anymore. Still, when events like Pat's Ocean Shores golf tournament rolled around, we invited them, and they came—since they knew others would be there and they wouldn't be thrown with "the crazy Boones" exclusively. They loved us, you understand, but still figured we were slightly "touched."

We prayed that Jim and Carole would find the great joy in God that we'd found, but we never talked much with them about the Holy Spirit, for fear that we'd drive them further away.

We didn't push. We didn't pull. We only prayed—until God, as usual, accomplished what we'd been hesitant to try.

The change in the Hamptons began when Pat invited Jim to go with him to the Frasier-Ali fight, and he accepted the invitation.

Pat had assumed that Jim had read his book; but, on the night of the fight, learned that he hadn't. So he gave him one.

In the meantime, though we didn't know it, Carole Hampton was going through some of the torment I'd suffered, not for exactly the same reasons but with the same pain. And, as I'd done before her, she'd reached the end of her endurance. She was miserable, desperate and seeking hungrily for spiritual comfort.

So, when Jim came home with Pat's book, she read it first. She was so eager for the hope it offered, she wouldn't turn it over to her husband until she'd read the last page.

Then, since she knows my family, she called my youngest sister, Jenny, for counseling.

Was the baptism with Holy Spirit something that could only happen to "fanatics" like the Boones, was it a kookie sort of thing experienced only by eccentrics, or might it happen to *her*, too, and fill the void in *her* life? She was frantic to know.

Jenny told Carole what the Holy Spirit had done for her and hers as well as for Pat, me and ours. And Jenny said He could do the same for Carole. And Carole believed her!

She loosened her hold on Jim so that she could seize upon God, and, in answer to her earnest petition, she received the baptism of the Holy Spirit.

Pat and I, no longer acceptable in the local Church of Christ, had begun to attend an interdenominational church in the San Fernando Valley called Church on the Way, where the Holy Spirit was moving in power, and Carole began coming there.

One day, after a service, Jim began to question her.

"How'd you like that church?" he demanded.

"Fine."

"Do you think you're going to keep going there?"

"Oh, yes," Carole said. "It was *wonderful.*"

"And do you believe everything they believe there?"

"Yes," Carole assured him. She did.

"Ummm," Jim reflected. Then he posed the clincher.

"Do you speak in tongues?"

"Oh, yes," Carole smiled. "I do."

Well, with that, Jim almost fell out of his chair. He'd been trying to see just how far she'd committed herself to what he considered a peculiar doctrine at best and, having found out, he was shaken. He'd hoped—he'd almost been *sure*—she'd say "No" to the question about tongues.

Now though, with her new commitment in the open, Carole began to share her faith with Jim while he began to see a beautiful change in her. The contentment she'd found was too impressive to ignore.

Further, though he's one of the funniest people alive, Jim wasn't an irreligious man. Not at all.

In fact, he and Carole had been attending a Lutheran church and Jim had volunteered to revise the liturgy, making it more modern. (Pat had accused him of authoring a spiritual "Laugh-in.") They'd been dedicated to that church, but the emphasis had been on what *they* could do for *God*—so that it hadn't satisfied them spiritually.

Jim and Carole had walked a distance with the Lord already, so now, impressed by his wife's joy and seeking a closer relationship with God for himself, he, too, began attending the Valley church she liked so well.

The first time he went, he didn't think it was so bad.

As I've mentioned, Jim has a marvelous wit and on his first Sunday at the Church on the Way, the Lord gave our preacher, Jack Hayford, a sermon just loaded with humor.

Jim "dug" that.

But the next time he went to church with Carole, he heard some things he *didn't* like, and the third time, he heard a *message in tongues and an interpretation.*

That tore it!

Jim admitted that the unknown tongue sounded like a genuine language, not wild babbling—that, in fact, he believed it *was* one—and that the interpretation seemed genuine.

Nevertheless, it shook him; he said he wanted to get out of that service and never go to that church again.

So that night, while Carole went back to church, Jim went to a Hollywood party with no premonition that God was leading him into a corner. But he soon found out that he was trapped.

For at the party people asked him, "Where's Carole?" When he told them, "She's at church," friends asked, "What church?"

Then, as Jim hesitantly *told* them what church, to his amazement, they really seemed *interested*; they asked more questions, and he gradually found himself describing the worship services and underscoring the Bible example and authority for supernatural power in a church today!

Like Johnny Cash ending a concert with an altar call, Jim was amazed by what he was doing, because he'd never in his life witnessed for Christ to a group of Hollywood party-goers. However, the action brought him to a moment of truth.

For by the time Jim left the party, he was convinced: he either had to experience the new power in Carole's life for himself—or escape it entirely!

"I can't continue to stand on middle ground," he told himself.

Therefore, that very night he got Carole out of bed and went to the Hayford's for prayer and guidance where, for roughly three hours, Jack wisely listened to Jim argue with *himself*, questioning, seeking yet fearing.

Did he or did he not want the baptism of the Holy Spirit? Jack smiled at Jim's writhing indecision. One of the scriptures Jack read was Jesus' statement, "Blessed (or happy) are those who hunger and thirst after righteousness—*for they shall be filled!*" [1]

At last, after reading scriptures with Jack and praying diligently, Jim knew that he was as hungry for God's extra spiritual gift as Carole had been—and with great joy he received it!

When I say "with great joy," that's exactly what I mean—for as Jim received the baptism, he was not only speaking in a new language but he was *laughing*!

Speaking through bursts of deep, delightful, soul-washing laughter, he had no idea what he was saying, but Jack, from his seminary studies, knew.

"Jim," he told our friend, "you're saying in Greek, *'I am happy. I am happy,* over and over again."

What *truth* there was in the phrase! Hadn't Jesus promised that very thing? [2]

Jim was so filled with peace and joy, he was happier than he'd ever been in his life.

And since that night he and Carole have grown spiritually by leaps and bounds!

Not everyone in the entertainment industry who's searching for spiritual fulfillment has received the Spirit, but seekers increase in number every day.

A famous black singer, who'd strayed from God, appeared on the "Oral Roberts Show," and it stirred in him a desire to once again walk with the Lord. Then he came under the Lord's power again at a Kathryn Kuhlman meeting, and now he and his wife are praying for their own Spirit-filling.

Another singer who has starred on Broadway and in movies and night clubs rushed into a locker room on a recent night when Pat was dressing for a charity basketball game.

"Pat," he asked, with his great, booming voice indifferent to other persons in the room, "how do you get the Holy

Spirit *in* ya? There are some things in my life I don't like—and I want Him to *change* 'em!"

"All you have to do is ask," Pat told him.

A lovely young actress we've known for several years, who goes from one major picture to another, was upset by her private life, though for a time she wouldn't admit this even to herself.

After I'd shared Jesus with her at some parties she asked to read Pat's book. We encouraged her to study the Bible and, at last, to ask for baptism both by water and Spirit. The Lord baptized this lovely girl in His Spirit; Pat baptized her in water in our family pool, and, almost immediately, God began to show His power in her life.

Because she's beautiful, she'd dated a number of prominent men and had been active in the Hollywood party life—she was afraid she'd be too weak to escape from this life-style. She felt she'd need someone who would understand her new commitment.

The night after her baptism in our pool, she attended a Bible study session at our house, and the next night on a blind date—something she'd normally have turned down—she met a devout Christian man who "happens" to be in show business. They quickly became spiritual companions and are now engaged to be married.

"I never thought I'd end an evening with a man *on my knees praying!*" she said later.

She has not only been surprised to find herself in prayer but to find herself *enjoying* it more than she'd previously enjoyed "a night on the town."

God, who loves each of us so much, has shown His love for this girl in a particularly wonderful way.

For example, she and some other celebrities were flying from the East to California. She prayed, "Jesus, I don't want to sit next to someone I don't know," but the stewardess sat her next to a strange man on the flight. As he leaned over and offered her some gum, she thought, *Here we go again!*

But a second later, when the stranger offered her something to read, she learned from the literature that he was a leader in the Campus Crusade for Christ organization, so their flight together became an occasion for spiritual growth rather than the "battle of the sexes."

Before her experience with Jesus, this girl had been deeply but unwisely infatuated with a major show-biz executive. She'd found him hard to resist.

But, when he came to see her after her baptism, she discovered herself free from his magnetism.

"It's all over," she began to tell him.

Being the typical Hollywood male, he couldn't believe it and tried to prove her wrong.

Just then, *her phone rang in another room* and she ran to answer it. Her new and treasured friend, the Christian man she'd met on the blind date, was calling.

The telephone's ring had been providential! 3

After the call, when the girl returned to the room where she'd left the show-biz executive—*she found him gone.* God hadn't allowed her to be tempted beyond her strength. 4

These entertainers—the talented, beautiful, charismatic people who've turned to God—are no less gifted and attractive now than they were before their spiritual transformations. If anything, they're *more* attractive, because they now have an inner peace which adds to their beauty.

Nor have they become bored—or boring!

Instead, their lives are filled with adventure and excitement as they witness daily the exciting miracles of God.

You'll often see them at the center of exciting discussion groups!

Many of these new believers are "baby Christians" and they'll continue to stumble and fall, but they've all met the one Person who will help them up and put the pieces of their lives together. So they *can* have a real purpose for living—to glorify Christ—but they still have "free will." They can choose to walk with Him or turn their backs on

Him again. The difference now is—because they are the children of God through receiving Jesus as their Savior—God will chasten those he loves. 5 They won't really enjoy the old life anymore and God will teach them discipline.

Don't look for *perfection,* but praise God for the beginning of *new life in Hollywood.*

This Hollywood has an interesting future, not so much as a glamour center, (though I have nothing against glamour), but as a center from which talented people will use their gifts for God.

In the past, movie stars have influenced dress, music and love-making. I pray that in the future Hollywood may exert an even greater influence on souls.

Let me encourage you to keep praying for Hollywood stars by name. I have prayed for one star for three years and just recently she has committed her life to Christ and is constantly seeking a closer walk with Jesus. She could have a tremendous influence in the lives of other "stars" for whom I and many others have prayed for several years. Just remember *all things are possible with God—even in Hollywood!*

Meanwhile, though, it's scarcely "The City of God."

With four daughters to guide, Pat and I are acutely aware of the so-called "New Morality."

And in the next chapter, I'll tell you how we confront it and why we believe that our daughters will survive it.

19
Dirt On The Rug

"Daddy," blonde, blue-eyed, dainty little Debby asked, "is it wrong to say_____?" One of the foulest obscenities imaginable popped from her cherubic mouth. *Our seven year old daughter!*

Her face was fresh-scrubbed for church, and in her best yellow dress she looked like a new-blooming daffodil. But the word she had used was strictly from the gutter!

Her sisters, also scrubbed for church and wearing their best yellow dresses, promptly joined in the inquisition.

"Yes, Daddy," Laury, our youngest, demanded, "can we say_____? That's what the boys up the street say!"

And with that, each of our carefully nurtured daughters let go a string of obscenities, echoing all the words they'd heard "up the street!" The Free Speech Movement had come to the Boone dinner table with a cascade of shocking sound which, for the moment, left Pat immobilized with his mouth hanging open.

The incident, funny in retrospect, happened seven or eight years ago while our daughters were still children, and it illustrates the fruits (good and bad) of an open society.

Pat and I have always tried to be completely honest with our children while we've encouraged them to be honest with us. We've claimed to welcome all their questions—about sex, the meanings of words, bodily functions, politics, religion and everything else—and we've done our best to answer truthfully.

Complete honesty within the family circle, we've learned, builds bridges across the generation gap. And what an unpredictable adventure! For the parent, it can be like walking a tightrope—blindfolded!

The first time your baby girl tosses off a four-letter word between the main course and dessert, it may do something to your digestion!

I was in the hospital (fortunately, perhaps) recovering from mononucleosis when Pat faced the challenge, assisted by Maureen, his very proper English secretary (and my dear friend) who was staying at the house during my illness to help take care of the girls.

It was Wednesday night, so Pat and the children were going to prayer meeting after dinner, and Maureen had bathed and dressed the girls for the occasion. Fresh from the tub, they were visions of sweet innocence when their father, running late as he often does, dashed through the front door and headed for the dining room.

"Come on, girls," Pat summoned his daughters. "We'll have to eat in twenty minutes if we're going to get to church on time. So tonight let's have no talk at the table. Just eat your dinner, and we'll talk in the car. All right?"

Though the girls were bursting with conversation, they complied at first and, for a time, only the clatter of knives and forks broke the dining room quiet.

Pat had every right to feel smug as he noted how docilely his four little visions of innocence obeyed his paternal injunction.

Then one of the visions, either completely forgetting his instructions or unable to contain her curiosity another second, dropped the bomb.

"Daddy," Debby demanded, fixing Pat with an angelic stare, "is it wrong to say_____?"

If Pat had had food in his mouth just then, he might have choked. As it was, he froze, while Maureen simply slid under the table, her face the pulsating red of a traffic warning signal.

Meanwhile the girls were bombarding Pat with such a torrent of obscene language that he was beginning to hope he was dreaming. The scene, he thought wildly, had to be a nightmare! Those sweet little sisters and that terrible language!

It was real though, and Pat, having been blessed with the responsibilities of parenthood, was going to have to deal with it. As he sat at the table trying to figure what to say or do, his sense of humor made the decision for him—and he burst out laughing.

Maureen, for her part, was so embarrassed that she was about to cry, but Pat was laughing so hard that he was shaking and tears were running down his cheeks.

On the other hand, the girls didn't get the joke and were beginning to eye their father suspiciously. After all, they'd asked him simple, straightforward, reasonable (from their way of thinking) questions which he, according to past promises, was obligated to answer.

"All right, girls," Pat finally said, pulling himself together and praying for wisdom, "it *is* wrong to use those words."

That wasn't so hard, he was congratulating himself. *Now we can finish our meal.*

The girls, however, weren't ready to let the subject die. "But, Daddy," Debby persisted, "what does_____ mean?"

"Yes," her sister chorused, "what does it *mean*?"

Pat's mind was racing. He'd told them in the past that

he'd never dodge a single one of their questions, and he wasn't going to. But how in the world, he wondered, should he answer them?

"Now wait a minute," he said with as much dignity as he could muster. "Let's quit saying those words right now. And then listen to me.

"There are some words that have *no* good meaning, because they are made up by someone who wants a dirty way of saying something. So, in themselves, they don't serve a good purpose and don't *have* a good meaning. Do you understand?"

"Yes," his daughters nodded, "but what does_____ _____mean?"

"I'm trying to explain," Pat said somewhat frantically. His thoughts were churning as he tried to decide how he could explain to his daughters what the obscenities with which they seemed infatuated meant.

"Well, first of all, there are certain words ladies never use, so you can just put them out of your minds. Just forget that you heard these words. And if those boys use them in your presence again, you come to me and tell me, because I'll want to talk to them. In fact, you can tell those boys that if they ever use such words around you again, I'll speak to their parents about it because they souldn't be using such language themselves."

"Yes, but what does_____mean?"

Now Pat knew that he couldn't beat around the bush. He'd have to define that particular word right then and there, or his daughters might not bring him later questions.

So he said to the children, "Let me put it this way: If we had guests over, would you say to me right in front of everyone, 'I have to have a B.M.?' "

Stunned silence.

Then, "oh, no." The little girls were horrified at the very thought of such crudity. "Is that what_____ _____means?"

174

"That's close—very close," Pat told them, and that was the end of the discussion. The children themselves were not only embarrassed by one of the terms they'd found so intriguing, but their curosity was satisfied—so Pat was spared further interrogation.

This is the way it has usually gone at our house when the girls have asked ticklish questions. Whatever the area of their immediate interest, we've told them enough truth to satisfy their curiosity without forcing additional information upon them. I'm convinced that when a child is force-fed more than she wants to know, she may get mental indigestion.

Of course, over the years, the girls have come to us (usually to me) with many questions about terms, phrases and natural processes which we've discussed candidly and in more detail.

And some of these discussions have become very precious experiences which my daughters and I are grateful that we shared. For example, I prepared each girl for menstruation by explaining to her the changes that were to take place in her body and how important these changes would be in God's plan for her life. We talked about both the physical and spiritual aspects of womanhood and the wonderful years that were about to begin.

Then I told each girl, "At school, you may hear some of your friends talking about these things, but be careful that you don't say anything to them that will rob them of moments like the ones we've just had together.

"A conversation like this between a mother and daughter is a precious experience for both. The time we've just spent has been a wonderful time of sharing, and I know you wouldn't want to deny one of your friends a similar time with *her* mother."

In this way, I've explained to the girls that certain subjects aren't suitable for general conversation; not because they are "dirty," but because they are too personal and precious to be debased through careless talk.

The one time my mother tried to talk with me about my body and the various maturing processes, I was embarrassed; and I think she was too, because we hadn't talked so intimately before. Our mutual embarrassment robbed me of a wonderful moment with my mother. Both of us were the poorer because we failed to appreciate the opportunity for loving conversation.

While I was at West High, the home economics teacher showed a film explaining human reproduction, and I blushed bright red, even in a class of all girls! In my early years I honestly and truly thought that if I kissed a boy I'd be pregnant (which at least had the good effect of keeping me from kissing boys too soon).

I wouldn't want my girls to be as uninformed as I was at their respective ages (and they're not!). Yet, on the other hand, I don't want them to be so glutted with cheap talk about sex that they'll become casual about it. God gave man and woman the potential for a beautiful relationship, yet, in order to achieve it, we must understand that sex is a gift from God.

Sometimes the girls hear a fact conveyed by a perfectly respectable word used in a way that sounds obscene, and we talk about that. I've told them, "God meant for everything to be good. But a person can misuse and abuse a good gift so that it becomes ugly. For example, our yard is made of dirt, and, treated properly, it gives us grass and beautiful flowers and fruit trees. On the other hand, if you get dirt on your shoes and delibertly track it into the living room, you leave ugly marks on the carpet because *you're misusing something God gave you.*"

Morally, things have changed a lot, even since *I* was a teenage girl. I know all young people now are faced with choices I never even heard of when I was in my teens. I keep hearing about "the new morality." As far as I can see, it's just "the old *im*morality." But, having given sin a catchy name, we tend to excuse it and thus make it that much harder for our children to resist.

These are such crazy, tragic days! Just this last school year, a fifteen-year-old schoolmate of our daughters boasted to them that she had not only spent a weekend with her eighteen-year-old boyfriend, but they had experimented to see *how many sins they could commit in an hour*! Nobody had to tell my girls that something was pitifully haywire! They've been praying for the girl ever since.

In every generation young people have experimented with sex, but when I was growing up they didn't openly brag about it. At least the girls didn't. Also, in the days before the "pill" and before instruction in contraception was a part of the high school curriculum, they worried more about pregnancy.

But now! A growing list of celebrities are glorifying unwed motherhood. Lots of others talk freely and openly about their affairs while condemning marriage as suffocating and archaic—and premarital sex is being packaged and sold as a positive virtue!

How can Pat and I *hope* to isolate our teenage daughters from the avalanche of sensual, sexual, immoral and antimoral influences all around us?

We can't. *We've decided there's no such thing as isolation for kids today.*

There's only *"in*sulation!"

20
Sex And Satan On T V!

In a newspaper interview a year or so ago, Los Angeles Superior Court Judge John Shilder said, "A big trouble with the world today is most people don't believe they can go to hell. They haven't been told often enough that there really is a devil."

Although Judge Shidler is married to actress Rosemary DeCamp, he wasn't directing his remarks toward the Hollywood contingent exclusively. Instead he was talking about society at large as viewed from the vantage point of a judge's bench.

As a matter of fact, Judge Shilder continued, "Many young people now barely believe in *death*, much less the devil."

In earlier times when the infant mortality rate was high and several generations lived under one roof, boys and girls were made aware of the frailty of life by deaths within their households. They saw baby brothers and sisters die, as well as great-uncles and grandmothers. Right in the next room!

So it's obvious they thought about eternity and God and the devil.

Now, however, most babies live, while the elderly are isolated from the young. Grandma and Grandpa are left behind in Iowa or they're snugly settled in "retirement communities" closed to youthful residents so that adolescents don't see their infirmities.

Further, when death does touch a family, it usually comes in a hospital, not in the back bedroom. So, to summarize Judge Shidler's thought, boys and girls have little occasion to ponder death on a personal level, much less the hereafter. And the devil, like "The Invisible Man," runs unnoticed and unchecked, creating heartbreak and havoc.

Our daughters believe in the devil because the Bible tells them he exists; Pat and I tell them he exists, and they see his works which tell them the same thing.

And, odd though this may sound to many of you, Pat and I consider the girls' knowledge of Satan part of their sex education. By this, I certainly don't mean that we think sex is sin. Far from it! *But the temptation to misuse it,* like the temptation to misuse any of God's gifts, *comes from the devil.*

When young people accept this, they don't become instantly infallible. Recognition of the devil is no chastity belt. Nevertheless, it's easier to avoid a pitfall if you know that it's waiting for you, and who dug it for you—and why.

Therefore, while boys and girls are learning the clinical aspects of sex, they should also be reminded that God and the devil each have a use for the exciting new urges they are experiencing.

As Richard Hogue points out in his excellent book, *Sex and the Jesus Kids,* " 'The devil made me do it' is no joke. In fact, Satan himself is the enemy—he's trying everything in the world to destroy this generation with sex—and, though the pressure may come from a thousand different directions, *Satan is the problem.* And you'll never get victory until you realize that *there is a devil* who's out to get you."

Parents should forewarn their children about Satan in the same way that they take them to their pediatrician for Salk antipolio vaccine, as an important protective measure. However, a warning about the devil isn't enough to guarantee a lifetime of immunity to transgression, any more than a single vaccination is enough to guarantee a lifetime of immunity to polio! Therefore, supplementary procedures (or spiritual "booster shots") are necessary in the form of further parental advice and control.

It's amazing how quickly little boys and girls discover that they *are* boys and girls—and that there's a difference!

I'm sure Cherry wasn't a day over eight years old when a boy no older then she was sent her a heart-shaped box of candy for Valentine's Day and a *ring*. He sent them all the way to England, too, because that's where we were at the time. While Cherry was still in first grade, she talked about being engaged!

Then, when Lindy was about the same age, she and Terry Taylor, Robert Taylor's son, had a big crush on each other. They swapped rings and really considered themselves romantically linked for years.

Of course, in every generation, children have probably talked about their "sweethearts" but, watching our daughters, Pat and I wondered why they and their friends were becoming so aware of the opposite sex so early.

Then one day it came to us: television! Not just the majority of the programs but the *commercials* have been selling sexuality to children almost from the moment sets were invented. The commercials are often more interesting than the shows, and almost without exception they preach that *the highest goal in life is to acquire "sex appeal."*

Toddlers, sitting before television sets, have it drummed into their little heads over and over again, subtly and otherwise, that *their ultimate obligation is to attract the opposite sex.*

Well, Pat and I weren't pleased about this realization, but we didn't get terribly excited until we saw sex being sold through an *oatmeal* commercial. That's when Pat blew up. Sex with your breakfast food?

Try to visualize this, if you don't remember it: From the television set, during a break in some program, a voice implores us (and our daughters) to eat more oatmeal. And all the while on the screen, a terribly sensuous blonde in a bathing suit is licking a spoon. In a close-up, she dawdles over her oatmeal, licking her lips and running her tongue along the spoon edge until the commercial looks like a scene from *Tom Jones.*

Well, watching that, Pat got so angry that, when he spoke at an awards dinner for an advertising agency, he really laid them low. I imagine they were sorry they'd invited him, but the idea of promoting oatmeal through sex infuriated him until tact wasn't important.

Agencies advertising oatmeal aren't the only offenders, however. What about the commercial wherein the camera focuses on a can of hair spray while, in the background, slightly out of focus, a couple slides giggling onto a sofa and disappears? What conclusions does a child draw from that? *She may eventually conclude that her only guarantee for successful living is to use products which will make her sexually attractive.*

I'm convinced that our TV generation has gotten more than radiation from the tube. A society in which *Playboy* is one of the three best-selling magazines is sex-oriented to a destructive degree.

The other day one of Laury's little friends, a girl not more than thirteen, remarked that her life's ambition is to pose for the *Playboy* center fold, which seems to prove everything I've been saying. Women's Lib notwithstanding, millions of little girls have been brainwashed to believe that to be a sex symbol is womanhood's supreme calling.

So, all this being the case, Pat and I have given our girls

"booster shots" to strengthen the protection against sexual license they received when they were "vaccinated" with knowledge of the devil.

In the first place, from the time our daughters were old enough to know what the word *date* meant, we've told them that they wouldn't be allowed to go out with boys alone until they were sixteen years old. And, since they've grown up with this understanding, they've accepted it.

Cherry has been dating for about a year now, so I asked her the other day, "Do you think you missed anything by not being allowed to date until you were sixteen?"

After thinking a moment, her answer was, "Nothing I wouldn't have wanted to miss."

In other words, she's been spared facing the problems and decision-making her friends had to contend with when they were thirteen, fourteen and fifteen and already dating heavily. She watched them go through periods of jealousy, fights with their boyfriends, and all sorts of emotional crises before they were at all prepared to handle these things.

Since Cherry started dating, she has found herself in occasional situations which have sent her running to me in tears. But, because she was slow to begin going out with boys, she was a little more mature, a little wiser, and a little better equipped to meet certain problems when they finally arose.

I know that gland-power can sometimes outmatch brainpower, even in the brightest, most level-headed teenagers, so I've urged each of my girls to put off her first kiss just as long as she can.

I don't tell her that kissing is immoral or unsanitary or anything like that, but I point out that a kiss is a very special mark of affection and, therefore, a girl's first kiss should be precious and memorable, not just a casual contact easily forgotten and signifying nothing.

By making our girls wait to date until they are sixteen— and by urging them to wait to kiss until their kisses will mean something enormously special, Pat and I believe we've given them one of the "booster shots" I mentioned earlier (administered with lots of love and togetherness!).

For their second "booster shot" we've given them plain, practical, straight-from-the-shoulder talk about the ills and downright stupidity of the so-called "new morality."

Some of the logic which seduces young people is as old as time.

The prevailing argument of a generation ago when people wore hats—"You wouldn't buy a hat without trying it on, would you?"—was probably a variation of Latin once effective in the top tier of the coliseum, "You wouldn't buy a toga, etc . . . ?"

While the plea, "Why should we wait when the bomb may drop on us tomorrow?" probably derived from a Dark Ages argument, "Why should we wait when we may be killed by the Northmen (the black death, a dragon, etc., etc.)?"

On the other hand, boys and girls are currently being assailed by new and sometimes deceptively subtle attacks upon premarital chastity coming from surprising sources. Not only do certain celebrities openly flaunt their infidelities, their affairs and their unwed parenthood, *some spokesmen for the church actually advocate sin*! Naturally they don't *call* it sin, but that's what it is just the same, if we can believe God's own Word.

In a recent story by Robert DiVeroli of Copley News Service, the Rev. William E. Genne, family consultant for the National Council of Churches, was quoted as saying that the family in American society will be strengthened by couples *living together for a time before marriage* "to make sure their marriages will work."

Amazing, isn't it? A statement like this attributed to a churchman!

Confronted with such an argument stemming from such a widely respected source, it's small wonder so many young people sneer at the "Puritan ethic." Nor is it any wonder that parents who try to defend old-fashioned virtue often feel disarmed before they've begun to fight.

How can a mere mother answer the wisdom of the learned and ordained Rev. Genne? For that matter, how can she sell her old-fashioned conviction in contest with the glamorous life-styles of certain jet-setters and movie stars?

Fortunately, I have two strong allies in my campaign to teach our daughters decency.

The first is example. By looking around their own community, the Hollywood-Beverly Hills complex, they can see what happens to girls who abandon morality for pleasure or ambition. The entertainment community may not be more sinful than any other, but, thanks to eagle-eyed columnists, its transgressions are easier to examine. So by reading the papers (trades and dailies) and keeping their wits about them, Cherry, Lindy, Debby and Laury can observe the wages of sin.

A year or so ago, a beautiful young actress became the much-publicized mistress of a married man. They made no bones about their relationship, even though he had a wife and children. The actress' career was on the upgrade. I think she honestly loved her lover and thought he'd get a divorce and marry her.

As it turned out, he got his divorce, but he married someone else, while his discarded mistress, trying to restore her own ego perhaps, took another lover. Then another. She slept one night not with one but with two singers!

Now when columnists report her "dates," readers laugh; and when producers cast important pictures, they pass her by. Once a girl with great star potential, today she's become a joke to everybody, including her original seducer.

I've never discussed this particularly bleak Hollywood chapter with my daughters, but if they aren't aware of its unhappy heroine, they *are* aware of other girls whose careers have paralleled hers. They are aware of girls who, after dozens of interviews on "casting couches," suddenly realize that they've never gone before cameras and probably never will. Unwittingly, these girls have become *unpaid prostitutes,* the "models" and "starlets" who drearily entertain actors and studio executives with free evenings.

I am very sorry for these girls. The example they set is a telling argument in favor of chastity which, I pray, is not lost on other girls.

Where my own daughters are concerned, my second great ally in my campaign for old-fashioned virtue is, naturally, *Pat.*

As their dad, he gives the girls a man's point of view which most men still maintain—no matter how they lie to the girls they're out with!

21
Daddy To Daughter

Often when I've disciplined one of the girls, I've reminded her, "Look, God has given us an order of things. Your Daddy is subjected to God. I'm under subjection to Daddy, and you children are under subjection to both your father and me until you're old enough to have authority.

"As long as Daddy is around, I do what he says, though I sometimes disagree with him, because I know that God intends him to be the head of the house. In the same way, when you mind me or your father, you do it not only to please us but because you know you please God when you obey your parents."

The husband of a friend of mine stated the case bluntly when his children whined just once too often, "Why do we have to, Daddy?"

"Because," he said, "next to God, I'm boss. That's why."

In other words, in households which follow God's design for family life, the husband is the boss, and for that reason, if for no other, our daughters would pay attention to what Pat says.

When they were very young, even though Pat was gone most of the time, I established a relationship between him and the girls that kept order in our home and communcations open. Everytime we made a decision I would ask the girls, "what would Daddy want us to do?" Then when Pat would come home from a singing tour, a relative stranger again, they recognized that he was at the top of our household chain of command.

Of course now we're together more and I'm so glad that in these *teen years* they have God's order in our home—both by teaching and example.

However, when Pat talks with them about sexual temptation and the sad results of sin, they listen not so much because he's their father—as they do because he's a man. They know that he not only looks at sex from a man's point of view but that he has confirmed his opinions by talking with men he knows.

Now *some* girls can write off *their* father's pals as a bunch of old fogies and squares or, possibly, as so "over the hill" themselves that they only know about sexual sin through hearsay and vague recollection. However, our daughters know that the men who share Pat's views aren't a bunch of overweight, undersexed fuddy-duddies. Not by a long shot!

Many (or most) of them are Hollywood's swinging glamour boys who may not always live by the precepts they hold but who, nonetheless, still have old-fashioned respect for "good" girls and earnestly hope their daughters won't ever behave the way their mistresses do.

With so many young people not only living together without marriage but actually being *commended* for it, with various experts and pseudo-experts arguing that no man and woman should expect *a lifelong relationship,* I'm glad I have Pat to explain to our daughters just what marriage is all about and why no "reasonable facsimile" is just as good.

He tells them:

"In the first place, when you consider what sort of sex life you'll have, you have to decide whether you're going to accept or reject the Bible and its teachings. See, the Bible very clearly tells us that God intends each man to have one wife, for him to take care of her, and for the two of them to be true and faithful to each other.

"In God's plan, a man and wife become as one flesh. You should no more divorce your mate than you'd remove half your body! So, if you *believe* that—and think of marriage as a permanent arrangement, you'll enter it only after you have given the step a *lot* of careful thought. Then, even in the face of temptations and in the unhappy times most couples eventually experience, you'll ask God to keep you faithful to your vows.

"Unfortunately, though, most young people don't know God and don't consider their sex activities any of His business. Yet, even *they* should realize that living together without marriage is a mistake.

"Look at it this way: you wouldn't consider going into a business venture with a partner, would you, without a contract of some kind? If you were going to commit yourself to a business deal, you'd want to be sure that your partner was going to commit himself, too, and that's why you'd probably insist that terms of the association be spelled out in a contract. At least, you sure *should!*

"Way back, under the law of Moses, it was possible for a man to get rid of his wife by simply saying, 'I divorce you.' A woman, on the other hand, couldn't get a divorce. She was her husband's property.

"Jesus was the only true Women's Liberator! He gave women new dignity and new rights! He not only forbade out-of-hand divorcement—the discarding of a wife simply because her husband was tired of her—but He told each husband that *his first earthly obligation was to his wife!* [1]

"Before the coming of Jesus, a wife was strictly at her husband's mercy—and I'm pretty sure no modern girl would want to revert to *that* arrangement.

"I imagine that almost every girl who enters into a sexual arrangement, or 'trial period,' today does so with the expectation that she and her partner will live together as equals so long as their love lasts, believing that, if it ends, they can walk away from each other with 'no harm done.'

"Such an alliance, however, can't compare with marriage. In fact, trying to compare unlicensed sex with marriage is like comparing apples to oranges. They just aren't the same things at all.

"*Without a permanent commitment, there's little chance of a lasting relationship.* Perhaps I can explain best with an example. The other night in Las Vegas I was washing my car, a Rolls Royce convertible, at an all-night station. I was washing it at night after my shows because the Las Vegas temperature was only about 110 degrees then, not 120 like it had been during the day.

"A fellow working at the all-night station thought it was kind of funny that a guy driving a Rolls was washing his own car, but I said I *liked* taking care of it, and the two of us got into a conversation about how much we enjoyed caring for our automobiles.

"As we talked, I remembered something, and I told the fellow, 'I enjoy this Rolls, but it's no prettier to me than a '50 Chevy Shirley and I owned when we first married and lived in Texas.'

"That Chevrolet—it was two-toned green with white sidewall tires—had about 80,000 miles on it. The tires were thin, and the seat covers were giving way. But it never needed a major overhaul. It was *our* car, Shirley's and mine, and we took good care of it because we knew that if anything happened to it, we'd be walking and riding the bus.

"I'm sure other people didn't see the beauty in our car that I saw, but I loved it. It was my pride and joy because I'd put so much of *myself* into it. Its good qualities filled me with such pride that I didn't even notice the bad ones.

"Well, I think that car can teach a lesson to every young

couple planning to move in together without marriage. Without marriage, you won't see the good qualities in your mate that you'd see if you'd committed yourself fully to the relationship. If, through marriage, another person becomes yours forever and ever, and there's no easy way to walk off, you'll give more of yourself to that person.

"You'll be less likely to notice defects in that person and more likely to find good qualities, because that person will have become *a permanent part of yourself.*

"When I think of so-called trial marriages or sexual relationships without marriage, I visualize a supermarket where a guy can walk in, look over the goods, and sample whatever looks tempting before he buys.

"He may open a can, take a few bites, and then put the product down, because something on another shelf looks more inviting. If a box of cereal tempts him, he opens the box, eats until he's satisfied, and throws the rest away.

"Actually that's the kind of relationship young people are advocating when they glorify trial marriage. Or 'the new morality,' they call it.

"They're pushing for a society wherein each person helps himself to a little of this and a little of that without buying a thing. Then, when he's had enough, he leaves the broken boxes and half-consumed products to the next shopper who may buy what's left and take it home or do a little more sampling and walk away *with no commitment to pay for anything.*

"I don't have statistics on how many premarital relationships lead to anything permanent, but I'll bet you my Rolls that very few do. (I'd never bet that '50 Chevy!)

"There can be no permanent relationship *until two people permanently commit themselves to one another!* One major feature of marriage is the lack of alternative.

"I think the motion picture *Love Story* was basically destructive because it encouraged young people to move in together with the thought that everything is going to be beautiful.

"As I said, a girl usually looks at a premarital alliance this way—romantically. She thinks (and probably the guy tells her), 'We don't need a license. We'll just grow together and love each other.'

"Well, the guy may start out thinking that way, but, fair or not, he'll probably get tired of the restrictions, and pretty soon he may have another affair on the side. Then gradually—and he'll find lots of reasons for this—he and the girl he lives with will have big problems, and he'll move out, leaving her wounded and vulnerable. A perfect target for the next man.

"I'm around these guys all the time and hear what they say, so I know what I'm talking about.

"Even with a commitment like marriage, a couple will find it rough, very rough, to get through certain periods and, if there's no marriage at all, it's irresistably easy to give the whole thing up.

"When young people ask, 'But if we aren't happy together, *shouldn't* we separate?' I say, 'No.' For not even the happiest of happily married couples have been happy every day of their married lives. Shirley and I can vouch for that!

"But, with God's help, it's easier to stick to your commitment and work out your marital problems than it is to run away from them. In this connection I remember an actor who was an enormously popular star in the 1930s and '40s and whose wife was an important star until she retired following the birth of their now-grown children.

"They'd been married for almost a generation when, one day about ten years ago, he announced, 'Something's wrong. I'm not happy.'

" 'What makes you think you are supposed to be "happy".'? his wife, a sensible lady, replied smartly. 'All you're supposed to be is doing your best.'

"Their marriage has continued and, though I can't guarantee how happy he is, I can almost guarantee that he's happier than he'd be if he'd left home in the pursuit of pleasure with a girl half his age.

"I was on the 'Virginia Graham Show' recently with an actress who told all the viewing world that her teenage daughter was living with a man and that, if things worked out, they would get married. The mother not only thought this was great, but other people on the show sort of went along with her.

"Finally, Virginia asked me what I'd do if one of my daughters came to me and said she wanted to move in with some guy. I said, 'Well, I'd ask her to come down with me to a quiet part of the house where we could have a talk. I'd tell her exactly how I felt about what she was planning to do, and then I'd turn her over my lap and *spank the fire out of her.*'

"When I said that, the audience erupted in a roar of applause. I got the feeling that the audience, at least, was *wanting* somebody to say just what I'd said: That, if a girl was thinking like a selfish child, she should be treated like one.

"To return to the example of the supermarket, every housewife who shops for her family's food knows how produce that's been handled a lot gets bruised—until nobody wants it.

"If a woman shopper sees another housewife pick up a tomato and squeeze it and put it down, she probably won't pick it up at all. When a product has been mauled by several people, nobody wants it.

"The sexual smorgasbord in which some of our young people are indulging themselves will not only produce few if any lasting relationships; it will leave tragic debris of trampled emotions and broken lives.

"When I see young men and women pairing off with others who've had one affair after another or even one *marriage* after another, I'm puzzled by their taste because I doubt that anyone of them would want to be operated on by a brain surgeon whose past several patients had died on the table. Would you?

"In other words, I'd rather be part of a *success story* than move in with the most beautiful girl in the world who'd been party to a string of brief love affairs.

"I think of an apparently irresistible actress (no I won't name her) who's married and divorced three times and who's been involved in who knows how many other relationships, none lasting. And I have to conclude that, no matter how fascinating she is, there's *something basically lacking* in this girl. Why, I wonder, would anyone want to give himself to someone who is such a chronic loser?"

Pat says a lot more on the subject, but that's the crux of it; and, as you can tell, he's a pretty convincing advocate when he pleads the case for virtue. Meanwhile, the greatest argument I can present for constancy is my own experience.

Since Pat and I could never conceive of an alternative to being married, the girls have watched us meet difficulties and overcome them *within the framework of marriage*. Yes we've encountered grievous problems and have gone through periods when we weren't sure that we'd ever be happy together again. Nevertheless—and I thank God for this—we couldn't imagine ourselves divorced; so, instead of turning to an attorney, we turned to prayer.

If a wife has the "out" of divorce always available, it makes it easier for her to see the faults in her husband, and vice versa. A happy marriage isn't the easiest thing in the world to achieve, but it's much easier to come by than a happy but illicit affair.

In our house, *sex* is a good word! But we discuss sexual temptations openly as a trap set by the devil. Our daughters know that if they walk out from under the protection of God, the devil will quickly take over because he's always present and eager. But they also know that if they commit themselves to Jesus, He will bless them wonderfully. And most encouraging of all, He won't *let* them be tempted with more than they can bear.

22

The Devil At Your Door

We haven't had a Halloween party for the past three years, nor have we or our daughters been to one.

I imagine many (maybe most) people will consider our attitude toward Halloween downright crazy, but it came as a part of a package of changes in our lives when we established our new relationship with God.

We Boones didn't give up witches, ghouls and fortune-telling because we don't believe that dark, disembodied spirits haunt the world.

We gave them up because we *do*.

We firmly believe in the power and existence of evil spirits, and we don't want to invite them, even inadvertently, into our home.

This sounds medieval, I'm sure, but it's actually biblical. We have God's own word for the existence of spirits, good and bad. [1] The Bible specifically warns us against the legions of darkness seeking our souls; at the same time, it tells us that angels minister to us and that we may entertain angels unaware.

Today precognition and extrasensory perception are accepted to such a degree that they are subjects for study by major universities, and the Russian government is allegedly experimenting with ESP *as a means of transmitting official messages!*

Across all strata of society, interest in astrology, the psychic and even witchcraft has reached "craze" proportions, while phenomena which are inexplicable by rules of natural law are being reported almost daily. Sources ranging from the widow of Bishop James Pike to prominent television and motion-picture stars are claiming fascinating, supernatural experiences, contacts with ghosts, strong evidence of reincarnation, and so forth. Such accounts present an intriguing temptation to dabble in the occult. However, *such dabbling is dangerous!*

The Bible clearly condemns astrologers, soothsayers, diviners and persons dealing with "familiar spirits," [2] while at the same time it tells us that God, as well as the devil, deals in supernatural phenomena. Thus, the human mind is sometimes hard put to distinguish between the works of the two.

According to an article appearing in the July, 1968, issue of *Christian Life* magazine, David Stuart of Mission City, British Columbia, met an apparently extraterrestrial being on the Lougheed Highway near his home city on June 13, 1967.

Stuart, who was secretary of his church board at Mountain View Chapel, was at the wheel of his car, about to enter the flow of traffic, when he noticed a man standing by his left front window.

The stranger asked for a lift to Mission City, but Stuart, unaccustomed to picking up hitchhikers, drove away, leaving him at the curb.

Moments later, Stuart was startled to see the same man through his rearview mirror *sitting on the back seat of his car.* Speaking from nervous reaction, the driver asked his unexpected passenger whether he were a stranger in the neighborhood.

"I am a stranger unto many," the hitchhiker reportedly answered.

That was the end of the conversation until Stuart, reaching his turnoff, told his passenger he would have to leave him.

"I want you to remember one thing," the strange man said. "Jesus is coming soon."

When Stuart looked back to reply, *he found the back seat empty.* even though he hadn't stopped the car.

Arriving at church, he found the car doors locked, just as they had been when he began his adventure, so he concluded that he'd entertained an angel unaware.

The *Christian Life article added that several similar incidents have been reported.*

Don Tanner, religion editor of *The South Bay Daily Breeze* (Torrance, California), in commenting upon Stuart's experience, points out that both demons and angels are extraterrestrial in that earth is not their natural habitat. After citing several biblical references to angels, especially a reference to guardian angels, [3] Tanner continues:

"Not all 'beings' are good, however. The Bible is also filled with incidents involving evil spirits. I have heard reports and seen evidence of demonic activity today.

"My father, an ordained Assemblies of God missionary, has seen some. It was during a prayer meeting years ago at his mission in the Congo. Most of those attending the service had fallen asleep: only the missionaries seemed to be in prayer. Suddenly my father saw imp-like creatures sitting on the heads of those asleep.

"Believing in the power of prayer to deliver those bound by evil spirits, he and others immediately began to pray against the forces of Satan. Soon the creatures disappeared; each of those afflicted awoke, and the prayer meeting was revived."

Supernatural phenomena unquestionably occur. So we face the problem: How do we determine the source?

When a person has supernatural knowledge, it must come from one of two sources, God or the devil; and, since Satan is very tricky, he often palms off his mischief as the work of the Lord. The person with psychic powers can be as fooled as anybody else, even believing that he is a tool of the supernatural God.

While Boston police were searching for the Boston Strangler, they sought help from every quarter, including two psychics. One was a famous Dutch "seer" who extended his help for a fee. The other was a local man who didn't function professionally as a psychic but who, because of his remarkable visions, volunteered his assistance to the police.

Both men stunned investigators by describing details of the crimes which only police assigned to the case and the murderer could know. In fact, the amateur psychic's knowledge was so precise that *he himself became a suspect.* Further, each psychic "saw" a strangler whose physical appearance and life-style he described to police in such uncanny detail it pointed like accusing fingers to two Boston-based sex deviates.

And that was the trouble. Though each had inexplicable knowledge of the murders, and though each described with supernatural accuracy the appearance and habits of a man he'd presumably never before heard of, the "seers" identified two different "stranglers"—*neither* of them the man who finally confessed to the murders.

Despite their good intentions and apparent supernatural powers, the psychics *complicated* the investigation in a manner which must have pleased the devil. So we come to a question: Just how should one gifted with psychic abilities react to and use the gift? Or *should* he?

Our youngest daughter, Laury, is acutely sensitive to the spiritual world. Through prayer she's received knowledge which was beyond her experience and intellectual capacity, which has proved to be 100 percent correct. When this has happened, we believe she's received a revelation from God. On the other hand, when she is exposed to an occult or demonic power, she's frighteningly susceptible.

Once at school, without taking what she was doing at all seriously, Laury joined some of her friends in chanting witchcraft invocations of some kind. Another time, she let a friend put her into a trance.

The results were alarming. Her personality changed completely for days. It was literally frightening to look into her eyes until, through much prayer, she escaped from the power she'd allowed to enter her life.

On another occasion, after she'd been reading an astrology book, though only in the most superficial way, she passed out on stage in Ogden, Utah.

I think some people, Laury among them, are just better receivers, more sensitive to unearthly influences, than the rest of us; and, because of this, they are in greater danger.

When Pat and I were discussing the validity and dangers of psychic experiences recently, he summed up his thinking this way:

"We know God gives some people special genius in music, some in mathematics, some in mechanical things. Some men have great physical prowess, far above the average, and some women, great beauty.

"That being true, we must assume that, within man's nervous system, there may be as much variation as there is in other facets of his being.

"I would guess that, when God bestows special gifts, He has a purpose in them and that He expects the recipient to use each gift to *His* glory.

"When Beethoven and Brahms and Handel wrote great oratorios and sacred music as well as symphonies and so forth, they were dedicating their musical ability to God, and He blessed them for it. Now, in the minds of men, they are immortals.

"So, persons are born with special spiritual sensitivity or unusual mental qualities and I think that God bestowed those characteristics for a purpose, and that the recipients are expected to yield the gifts back to Him—to use them for His glory.

"God has use for such talents, or He would never have given them. However, the devil can also make fantastic use of them, too. Satan is a monstrous deceiver who can lead the most conscientious person into mischievous misuse of his gifts from God. And don't think he won't pick on kids— he *loves* to!

"The person who is keenly attuned to spiritual influences, who is a superreceiver, should be especially careful to keep on a wavelength with God, checking *everything* by His Word, the Bible. Otherwise, the devil will claim him."

Shelby Grant, wife of Chad Everett, told in an interview how she was warned against evil spirits and how seriously she has taken the warning. She'd become casually interested in the occult, including the potential of seances (though she'd never attended one), when a friend gave her a completely unexpected warning. Out of the clear blue sky, he told her that she reminded him of his wife who, during a seance, had been seized by evil spirits. Shelby, he continued, should never under any circumstances attend a seance—lest the same thing happen to her!

Though Shelby appreciated the warning, she shrugged it off, until she received a second admonition—this one from a stranger. In London, with time on her hands while Chad worked in a picture, she had contacted an organization of spiritualists to ask for a schedule of seances. She thought she might attend one.

Shelby was shopping in Harrod's with the spiritualists' schedule in her pocket when a clerk addressed her. The clerk, a well-bred and sensible-looking woman, began by saying that she'd never done such a thing before, but that she felt compelled to sound a warning. Her mother, the clerk said, had attended a seance during which she was possessed by evil spirits who'd destroyed her.

The clerk added that, when she'd seen Shelby, she had felt an uncontrollable urge to warn her against a similar disaster.

"You must never attend a seance," she said.

Shelby, shaken, threw the spiritualists' schedule away. She says she'll never again *consider* attending a seance.

Some psychics definitely perform wonders—*but unless their powers come from the Holy Spirit and give glory to God, they and their followers are in danger.*

The Bible tells how an angel opened a prison door for Peter, [4] but it also tells how the witch of Endor *doomed King Saul's soul.* [5]

I'm sure that God often protects people when they dabble in things more explosive than they realize. But I ask myself, "Why take chances?"

When Pat was a child, a ouija board told him that he'd play center field for the Yankees and have eleven children. He probably has a better chance of playing center field for the Yankees than he does of having eleven children, but the ouija board—like the devil—was a liar.

By contrast, some fortune-tellers are startlingly accurate. Pat ignorantly and skeptically listened to one several years ago who foretold a great many things no one else would have predicted at the time—but which came true!

Nevertheless, we know now that he should never even have wasted time listening to her, for faith in fortune-telling negates faith in God. While it's true that the gift of prophecy is one of the gifts of the Holy Spirit, prophesying through the Holy Spirit is not the same thing as "telling fortunes."

A Spirit-filled prophet makes no claim of having special personal powers. Instead, he simply relays the Word of God. Few, if any, fortune-tellers take this attitude toward their precognition. If artifacts, crystal balls, astrology, cards, spirit writing or any such help is needed, "the prophet" is dealing with the *Devil*—because these things are condemned in the Word of God! [6]

Some months ago Pat was on the Steve Allen show with the popular psychic, Kenny Kingston. Kenny took Pat's ring, rubbed it, and began telling him things he could scarcely have learned through normal channels.

Then Steve asked, "Pat, are you a spiritualist?"

Pat said that he wasn't—but that *he did believe in spirits,* quoting several scriptures to make his point, including Hebrews 1:14. He quoted Ephesians 6, in which Paul warns that the Christian battle is not a flesh-and-blood one, but *against spirits without bodies.* Then he said, "Kenny, the thing that worries me about you is that *the Bible specifically condemns divination and dealing in familiar spirits."* Then he quoted Deuteronomy 18:10-12.

That didn't register at all; Kenny hardly seemed to hear Pat when he quoted Deuteronomy 18:10-12 anymore than biblical warnings about dark spirits and demonic legions registered with most people we read about in the Bible itself.

Even some missionary friends of ours came back from their post in Africa where they had encountered demonic activity, exclaiming that *they hadn't been prepared for what they confronted.* Members of the Church of Christ, they hadn't *believed* in such things. They were so innocent in regard to the powers of darkness that they themselves became temporarily possessed by demons. Only prayer freed them.

When they came back to this country to report to their home congregation, their leader publicly declared, "I want to confess my fault. I was unprepared to handle the problems I found. *I wasn't equipped to deal with them."*

But how many of us are?

We need to take the time and energy to read what the Bible says about the one Jesus describes as "the thief" who comes to "steal, and to kill and to destroy." [7]

Satan is *real*. As real as God Himself. The Bible says so. So ask the Lord to instruct, defend and arm you *for the battle you're already in.*

23
Free As A Bird

The night I went forward in church and begged God to take charge of my life, I meant every word of my plea. Yet, *if I hadn't reached the absolute end of my own resources,* I might have spoken with reservation because I had no idea what God would demand.

In the intervening months, I've learned that you can't *outgive God*; for, when you put your life in His hands, He gives blessings with a generosity beyond human desire!

On the other hand, though, He doesn't free you from problems. In fact, since Pat and I were filled with the Holy Spirit, our problems have multiplied, along with our willingness and power to confront them.

We fight with Satan every day. Once you establish a firm bond with Christ, you become a top-priority target for the devil, more than you've ever been before. Remember, it was only after Jesus was revealed as the Son of God and the Holy Spirit had descended upon Him that His trials began. And while I'm not comparing any human being to Jesus, His experience is repeated to some extent in every life wherein the Holy Spirit is operating.

It's possible, unfortunately, to receive the Holy Spirit, to reach a glorious peak of awareness of God, and then level off. The unwary too often say, "Well, that was wonderful," and then slide backward. Because, in faith, nobody stands still. You go forward or you fall away, though, unhappily, many people don't realize this. Paul understood the principle and referred to it when he spoke of the "fight of faith," a fight we must wage *hour* by *hour*. [1]

You can no more enjoy a full spiritual life on the basis of a single contact with the power of the Holy Spirit than you can live a vigorous physical life with only one meal. It's a fight, staying in tune with God. Yet it's so worth the winning!

Our problems since our baptism with the Holy Spirit come in all shapes and sizes, and sometimes provide a real spiritual workout! In the first place, some of our friends think we're crazy, which I'm afraid, is to be expected. By contrast, some people consider us godsends, combination miracle-workers, sages and horns of plenty, assigned to erase every difficulty from their own lives.

So now we not only have purely personal problems, bred within the Boone family; we also have problems of strangers who bring them to us because they're sure we can help. Numbers of people who believe that our experiences were valid conclude that, if they can just spend enough time with us, something magical will happen to make their lives sublime. Thus, our doorbell never stops ringing. Our house is not only on a Hollywood tour bus route, it's cited on a "movie star" map, so we are sitting ducks for all comers. We've had to stop seeing everyone that comes to the door because it got so out of hand. Now it can only be by appointment.

Occasionally we've attracted individuals who seemed definitely unbalanced, and that has been scary. For example, one guy who was by all visible evidence intensely hot-tempered, decided that God had sent him to us for money. He had genuine, drastic problems. He had a wife and children and had lost his job. When we tried to point him toward the Lord, he seemed glad to accept our counseling; but, then, he concluded that *we were his answer to hard times* and that we should give him money to move his family away from Los Angeles.

Well, we prayed about it quite a lot because, if God wanted us to give him money, we *wanted* to do it! Yet, we weren't sure that we should, because it seemed that our friend was missing the point of some great scriptural truths. He looked to *us* as a source of supply, not to God, who, we knew, would gladly lead him into his answers if only he'd get his focus off the Boones.

He was a car salesman, and we tried to explain that, if he'd rely on God, perhaps he'd sell ten cars in a day if he needed to, and, in the long run, earn more money than we could give him. Then God would become his *Father,* not just an impersonal something or another. When we tried to share this principle with our friend, he only became exasperated and answered, "If you were really my brother, you'd help me."

That notion became an obsession with him.

Meanwhile, we'd invited his family—a wife and five children—to dinner and to Bible studies several times, had actually given him some money, and we tried to convince his whole group of our genuine interest. Actually, the *time* we spent with that family should have proved our sincerity, because it would have been much easier to have given the man the money he wanted and said, "Go and good riddance—and may God forgive us." We were trying, though, to obey what we felt was God's will, to show him that by making God his source and his strength, he could go much farther than he would through a single handout.

The situation became very awkward at times. Awkward

and frightening—for the man was a stocky guy who sometimes showed real anger. However, he never actually threatened us and, eventually, he moved out of our lives.

Others, much closer to mental breakdowns, have come to the door, as have missionaries, sincerely convinced that we've been led into a false doctrine. Of course, since some of our own brothers and sisters in the Church of Christ believe this too, we've long since adjusted to that reaction.

People write letters full of Scripture, trying to explain away the miracles we've encountered, while one man went so far as to write a book, *Pat Boone and the Gift of Tongues,* to refute our convictions.

The author is a wonderful, sweet Christian man, and we love him. He's a Bible teacher at a Christian college who has been brought up in the Church of Christ, and he did his best through his book to prove that our experiences with the Holy Spirit simply hadn't occurred.

It seems so sad to me that such effort has been made in that direction. You can question doctrine or an interpretation of the Scripture, but you just can't refute *experience.* You can talk until the cows come home, but you won't convince a person that what happened to him didn't happen!

But on to other problems: The baptism of the Holy Spirit won't, in itself, protect you from sin, as I well know, because, since I received it, I've been tempted in one direction particularly: toward pride and self-righteousness. Therefore, I think the Lord has chastised me a little bit through differences with Pat.

All of a sudden now, when I think I'm tuned in with the Lord, Pat will make a decision I believe is wrong, and I'm set back by it. I know I've been right on some of these occasions, but, whenever I think I'm right, my confidence scares me. I wonder whether I'm being proud or arrogant. And I remember how *the Bible charges wives to be submissive to their husbands.*

So, when Pat and I disagree completely about a point, I tell him how I feel. But, after I've done that, I wholeheartedly back his final decision. That is the crux of my new attitude.

Were I to take the stand, "All right, go ahead and ruin yourself," I would ruin myself too. Right then and there. But when I take the attitude, "I don't believe you're right, but I'm submissive to you and will help you with what you want to accomplish," then I'm showing love. Almost inevitably, if Pat *is* about to make an error of judgment, God will show him his mistake, or God will turn the circumstances around so that good comes to pass after all.

It's not easy for a wife to be submissive, as God expects, and trust in the Lord to correct her husband. You'd better believe it's not! But, if a wife has enough faith to turn things over to God, she'll enjoy a happier marriage.

There've been times when I've foolishly refused to wait for God to take charge, with the result that Pat and I have had some pretty good arguments. There's quite a temptation to try and help God out and push through plans of your own while you're waiting for Him to do something.

But our heavenly Father won't be hurried. However, if instead of struggling, we'll be still and listen, He'll reveal His will. To wait upon the Lord is one of the most important practices of Christianity, for, when we refuse to wait, *we make such a mess of things!*

Instead of driving ourselves so relentlessly in hopes of doing God's will, we should rest in Him until the answers fall into place and we are freed from anxiety. That's the way to both peace and success. By taxing ourselves to stay a jump ahead of God's plan, we only run out of fuel.

Pat and I disagreed about the man I mentioned who thought we should give him money. The man claimed God had awakened him in the night and told him to come to us. He even quoted Scripture to prove his point. And, at first, Pat wanted to give him what he asked. On the other hand, I thought we should wait until God had shown us what was best. I was willing to let the man have the money—I have given more money to people, when I felt the Lord wanted me to—but I wanted to be sure that what we did would be *for the man's own good.* Incidentally, by that time he was working, but he wanted the money to "go to Hawaii as a missionary."

Pat prayed about the problem for quite a while. Several times he said, "Shirley, I'd rather give him what he wants."

Finally I conceded, "Pat, maybe I'm wrong about this, but why don't you call Harald Bredesen and get his advice before you do anything?" Harald Bredesen is a minister and a spiritual giant whose discernment Pat and I trust.

At that, Pat told me, "Boy, I got cold chills when you said that, because I just looked at my desk and saw a note, 'Call Harald Bredesen.' "

So Pat called Harald, and Harald agreed with me that giving the man money would be the worst thing we could do at that point. It could cripple him spiritually.

Pat, convinced at last, asked our friend to meet him at his office. When they met, Pat asked him whether he had a job in Hawaii. He didn't. Then Pat asked whether he knew anyone there, and again the answer was no. So Pat told him, "God awakened you to instruct *you.* If He'd wanted me to give you money, He would have awakened *me* with His message. If God wants you to go to Hawaii to preach, *He'll show you how to get there through your own efforts.*

"Are you sending your children to school? No. Do they have shoes? No. Right now you should take the money you have, which isn't enough to move your family to Hawaii, and buy shoes for your children. Put your children back in school. Then, if God wants you to leave Los Angeles, *He'll provide a way for you to do it.*"

The man couldn't accept Pat's answer and thought he and I were hypocrites. We didn't hear from our friend again for a long time, but eventually he sent word that everything was all right. I trust that it is.

Another man, actually a boy, attached himself to us for quite a while, in what seemed at first like a sincere effort to learn more about God, though I finally came to suspect he was just as dedicated to becoming a star of some kind. For he was terribly interested in the studios and once begged Pat to call the head of one and give him a reference.

At first we welcomed him and tried to minister to him because we could tell he was very lonely. However, the boy wouldn't do anything to establish either a social or religious life of his own away from us. Pat tried to get him to go to meetings of a young people's group at a dynamic local church, and though the boy went once, he wouldn't go back.

Finally he said he was going to the Midwest to his family, but one night, almost no time later, he was back on our doorstep. The boy wanted to come in and spend the night, but since Pat was out of town and I was alone with four girls, I wasn't keen about the idea. I kept thinking, *The nerve of this kid!*

However, I couldn't turn him away, so I let him in, gave him some supper, and told him he could sleep in our little guest house, but that the next morning he'd have to make another arrangement—like finding a job!

The next day he left. But pretty soon he was back, saying he couldn't find work. Through the help of a friend of ours, George Otis, he found employment and an apartment. However, the job didn't last, and, almost before I could turn around, he was back at our house. This happened again and again.

The last time we saw him, Pat gave the boy some money with the warning, "Don't contact me again until you've met with that church group I introduced you to at least twice to see whether God will work through them to provide the direction you need!"

The boy vowed that he would. Hopefully, he's keeping the vow.

Every time this mixed-up kid showed up at the door and I

fought an impulse to shut it in his face, I reminded myself how the Bible tells us we may entertain angels unaware. I'd ask myself, "If someone is in need—in need of clothes, comfort, anything—can I send him away? On the other hand, do we please God by encouraging weakness and turning a human being with perfectly good potential into a parasite?"

I'm still not sure where a Christian should draw the line. In the case of one family we encountered, I, rather than Pat, felt obliged to give them money, a sizable sum. God had not only dictated the amount to me, but also the date on which I should give it. So since I had my own money (a modest sum I'd inherited from Daddy), I gave the prescribed amount to the couple, and at the same time I gave advice.

I told them the money should only be used to pay their accumulated past-due debts and, reminding them of the biblical story of Ananias and Sapphira, warned them not to lie to the Holy Ghost. As far as I was concerned, I'd turned the money over to the Lord.

But, lo and behold, after the couple had only paid most of their debts, they used the cash for new clothes and health food. Maybe that was what God wanted them to do. I can't judge. Anyway, this young couple had decided to live by faith instead of by work, even though they had three children and the father was perfectly healthy. They were dedicated kids who said they'd received God's instruction *not to work*. In deciding how much to help the family, Pat and I wrestled with a terribly hard decision.

To make matters worse, someone called and told us that a widow was so worried about the couple's young children that she was giving them money she badly needed for herself. So, we fretted, "What should we do?"

As usual, I turned to the Bible for instruction and, the more I read, the more I became convinced that you're supposed to support yourself and your own to the very best of your ability. Even while Paul was ministering to others, he continued to support himself as a tentmaker. I read Scripture to the young husband and wife, but they thought I was a false prophet in their situation.

When the couple finally lost their house for failure to pay rent, the girl was pregnant again, so the whole crowd—father, pregnant mother and three little boys—came to me. I was so disturbed by this development that I called a friend of mine and asked her to pray with me before I met with our unexpected guests. While the friend and I were on the phone, our maid, who didn't know what was going on, told the kids that I was late for an appointment and couldn't see them.

They left, very despondent, thinking I'd turned my back on them, though, actually, I left money at our house for them in case they came back again. I told myself that I was leaving the money to tide them over until they could determine more clearly God's will, but, at the same time, I wondered whether I was really "buying them off"—paying them to move on rather than in with us.

For, I must confess, the thought of a pregnant woman and three little boys sharing our home was pretty overwhelming. We have a hectic, busy house already! That's why I called a very mature and very spiritual woman to pray with me and guide me before I went downstairs to my dilemma.

I think the kids moved up to Palmdale, and I'm afraid they still feel I was wrong. As maybe I was, for I'm as capable of being wrong as anyone else.

It scares me a little bit, thinking about that couple. I believe in the principle, "Give, and it shall be given unto you," and I know those kids had given up a great deal through their faith in God. They're really fine youngsters who'd been studying and growing and who'd done things for the sake of humility I'm afraid I never could have done. They'd been in show business. He'd had a hit record, but they'd let themselves be humbled until I'm sure God will make great use of them.

However, we disagreed over the business of living on faith. Only, *we* believe God wants work mixed with faith. Not "work"—earning righteousness through good deeds— but just good old bread-earning work!

As I said before, since we Boones encountered the power of the Holy Spirit, our problems have multiplied. And we certainly can't solve them all through "pat" formulas. Yet, we are never despairing, because, though human intellect often fails, *God never does.* We may not understand His plan, but we can trust it.

We've discovered that God doesn't imprison us with narrow restrictions. Rather, through the sacrifice of His Son, Jesus Christ, and the gift of the Holy Spirit, *our heavenly Father has set us joyously free!*

24

Lessons In Liberation

At 6 A.M. on February 9, 1971, I woke up in an earth-quake! And, as has so often been the case in moments of crisis, Pat was out of town.

The sensations induced by an earthquake are unique because, during a quake, the very ground upon which you've built your physical and material foundations becomes your foe. Like a horse trying to throw its rider, the earth heaves and tosses as though to rid itself of man and his works.

To see the walls of the home which has sheltered you waving like sheets on the clothesline tends to be unnerving. To find the once-solid floor no longer solid can be up-setting—literally!

Yet, when I was awakened on February 9 in my pitching and sliding bed and realized that a heavy quake was shaking Los Angeles, I didn't fall to my knees in terrified prayer. My spontaneous reaction as my feet hit the floor (which you may consider crazy) was to lift my hands and cry, *"Praise You, Jesus."*

Wild? You bet! But not in the way you're probably thinking.

My reaction was wild only because I had been a dedicated coward most of my life. Yet now I felt so calm, so full of peace, in the midst of physical danger which frightened some people clear out of Calfiornia. Yes, many people were so terrified by the quake that they sold their houses and *moved from the state.*

Fear, however, never entered my mind. Thrown by the shaking from wall to wall as I tried to run down the hall to the girls' rooms, I repeated again—still instinctively— *"Praise You, Jesus."*

Then I called, "It's all right, girls. It's an earthquake."

All right? An earthquake? I still find it hard to believe that I spoke so cheerfully and encouragingly without any trace of alarm. For, before the Holy Spirit filled my life, I was a mass of fears.

For example, I'd been a white-knuckled flier. Whenever I'd been on a plane, my heart had sunk in direct proportion to its rate of climb until, by the time it had reached cruising altitude, I'd become a package of pure panic.

I'd been afraid of public speaking, strangers, interviews, criticism, guilt and failure, and these had been only a *few* of my hang-ups. Psychologically, I'd been a mess, in bondage to dozens of terrors.

However, after my baptism with the Holy Spirit, I'd gradually discovered as various situations arose that I'd been freed from first one phobia and then another. I was no longer afraid of crowds or strangers or even failure, for I'd come to know that what might be failure in men's eyes is a triumph if it's ordained by God.

In short, as a Spirit-filled follower of Jesus, I'd been so freed from fear that *in an earthquake* I sincerely cried, "Praise You, Jesus."

Lindy and Cherry had been sleeping together with their door open, so the minute they awakened they saw the night light in the hall and could find their way to me.

Laury, too, could find her way, because she had a night light in her room. But Debby had been sleeping alone, in the dark with her door to the hall closed, because she had a bad cough.

But, as the Bible teaches us, the Lord prepared our way, for the only lamp knocked off a dresser by the quake fell in Debby's room and hit the floor in such a way that *the jolt turned it on!* So Debby , too, had light to guide her to the rest of us.

Because I'd awakened praising God, there was literally no place for fear in our house. The Bible says perfect love casts out fear. And what is perfect love? *God is Love. Jesus is love.* And surrounded by God's presence, the girls and I couldn't be afraid.

Many California children were in psychiatric clinics for weeks after the quake. I heard news reports that said the major problem was not the fear of the quakes, but the children's reactions to *the fear they saw in their parents.* The Lord had taken care of that problem for us.

Crawling onto my bed, we joined hands and sang, "Praise God from whom all blessings flow." Then we began praying in the Spirit. Meanwhile, still shaking along with our whole house, we could hear water in the swimming pool sloshing like water in a giant bathtub!

I think the *sounds* of the earthquake shocked me most. I'd never imagined the earth could make so much noise, like that of a train rushing under the house, while squeaks, rattles and crashes accompanied the roar.

Even so, we honestly weren't afraid, for what should we fear in the presence of the Lord? Until the last of the tremors which immediately followed the big quake was over, my daughters and I sat together on the bed, thanking and praising God and asking Him to lead us.

Surprised as I'd been at my reaction to the quake, I was equally surprised a little later to find myself sending the girls off to school. I've always been extremely protective toward my children and, in other years, I would have kept them at home for at least a day following the quake. I would have thought, *Suppose we have another one. Their school is old. Is it safe? I must protect my girls!*

But, after we'd climbed off the bed and surveyed the damage around the house (which, I'm glad to say, wasn't major), I felt no reluctance about sending them to classes. I knew *God* was with them.

I read Psalm 46, which offers beautiful comfort in time of a quake, poetically reminding us that God is our refuge and our strength. I've learned through experience that this is *absolute truth.* That God is a refuge and strength is no matter of theory with me but a matter of tested, proven fact.

As the girls left the house that morning, I reminded them, "If we have another earthquake, you know what to do. Get on your knees and praise the Lord. Get under a table or something, but get on your knees."

At the time of the quake, Pat was in Florida, but he was no more afraid for us than we were for ourselves, for he, too, was filled with the peace of God.

The peace of God does pass understanding. There's no two ways about it. Our freedom from fear wasn't explicable according to earthly logic, yet it was real.

Since receiving the baptism of the Holy Spirit, *I've lived with greater freedom, yet under greater discipline.* These statements sound contradictory but they support one another.

I've not only been granted freedom from fear, I've been freed from dozens—probably hundreds—of other debilitating insecurities and pressures through two disciplines:

1. I've disciplined myself to recognize blessing in seeming adversity.

2. I've disciplined myself to live under God's rules of order for the family and the world.

An excellent book, *From Prison to Praise*, written by an

air force chaplain who, before he gave his life to the Lord, was a bad soldier and a jailed car thief, taught me a great deal about blessings in disguise.

Jesus never promised His followers freedom from tribulation but, rather, that they would suffer trials and persecutions. In other words—freedom *in* tribulation! The Bible is full of stories about good, God-loving people who were sorely afflicted (Paul is a prime example) but whose sufferings gave them greater strength, greater endurance and greater patience, qualities which made them invincible.

Jesus, of course, gave us the most perfect example of a blessing in disguise.

Because He was man as well as God, He didn't want to be crucified anymore than any of us would want to be; so He prayed to His Father, "If it be possible, let this cup pass from me: nevertheless not as I will, but as thou wilt" (Matthew 26:39).

But if God had granted that prayer and saved Him from His terrible tribulation, *Jesus could not have achieved the greatest victory of all time* three days later when, conquering death and sin, He rose from the grave!

When you're hard pressed, think about that. Then praise God for the test through which He betters you.

David said, "Though I walk through the valley of the shadow of death, I will fear no evil; *for thou art with me"* (Psalm 23:4). That's something else to think about.

To the natural human mind, nothing is more fearsome than the valley of the shadow of death. But if we, like David, know that the Lord is with us, we too can be unafraid, confident that He'll take us safely to the other side.

When one is filled with trust in God and is aware that all things work for the good of those who love Him (Romans 8:28), *freedom from fear is automatic.*

Nevertheless, even when we have this trust, certain unpleasant pressures will continue unless we live according to the rules of order God has prescribed. For our good, the

Lord had decreed a divine order for man and woman, husband and wife, children, servants, for each of us—whatever our position.

So-called Women's Libbers militantly object to the place in society God has ordained for their sex, but, by so doing, they lose much precious liberty the Lord intended them to have.

As Larry Christensen points out in his book, *The Christian Family,* a divine order of authority and responsibility is revealed in the Bible which places Christ at the head of all. Continuing through the Scriptures, we learn that the husband should be subservient to Christ, the wife to her husband, and children to their parents.

However, in making the husband the head of the house, God *did not make the wife a chattel.* Genesis 2:24 leaves no doubt that a wife should be her husband's treasured companion, instructing, "For this cause a man shall leave his father and his mother, and cleave to his wife; and *they shall become one flesh"* (NASB).

At the same time, though, Genesis 2:18 tells us that God made woman as man's "helper" and not his supervisor or custodian. Over and over again the Bible indicates the proper relationship between the sexes. First Corinthians and 1 Peter speak of a wife being subject to her husband's authority, while, on the other side of the coin, Paul in Colossians 3:19 admonishes husbands to love their wives and not be harsh with them.

In 1 Peter 3:7 the inspired writer warns that unless the husband's relationship with his wife is godly, his prayers will be hindered!

Can you imagine a happier marriage than one in which these attitudes apply—one in which a kind and loving husband frees his helpmeet wife from the buffets which assault men and "liberated" women—by being head of the house and protecting her?

When a woman is submissive to her husband, she's

relieved of a lot of the hard, emotion-taxing decision-making, for this is the province of the head of the family. Meanwhile, *the husband is freed from criticism, nagging,* and counterproductive, independent action within the family circle.

As for single women, according to scriptual teaching, they should live under the authority of the church, which is commanded to care for them spiritually and materially, giving them the counsel and protection a husband should give to his wife.

Admittedly, few if any churches fill the role described in the Scriptures, with the result that single women are left to flounder and fight their way through the world as though they were men—*deprived of their freedom to be total women.*

At the same time, few families today enjoy the freedom found through applying God's rules for order.

However (I'm happy to say), Pat, our daughters and I have discovered recently through application how well the divinely proclaimed allocation of responsibility works and how much satisfaction it brings.

Jesus Christ is the heavenly authority above us all.

Next, Pat is decision-maker for our family and, as such, must be especially diligent to serve our Lord.

My place is to submit myself to Pat, while the girls are submissive to both parents.

Though I know—and I really do *know* it—that I've found new happiness and freedom through this Divine Order, I must frankly say that submission doesn't always come easy. For example, at times when I've told the girls they can't do something and Pat has overruled me, I've been furious, thinking, *What's my decision going to mean to our children if Pat's going to countermand it?* I've also thought, rather rebelliously, *Pat's wrong.*

However, I've prayed regularly for an obedient and submissive heart, and one day, as I prayed, God gave me the insight I needed.

"Shirley," His answer came, "you only have to be obedient. Pat doesn't have to be right. Continue to pray that you'll learn obedience, and trust Me to deal with your husband."

Once I felt a compelling need to fast as I prayed for a boy who was ill. I was convinced that God expected this of me. But Pat, as it turned out, didn't agree.

So at dinner that night he told me, "Shirley, I don't think you should be fasting, because you need your strength to keep up with this family. I wish you'd eat your dinner."

"But, Pat," I argued, "I know the Lord has put it into my heart that I should fast, and I don't think I should stop now."

Once again I thought, *Pat's wrong. God, what should I do?*

Then the Lord, as He does when we earnestly seek His will, gave me guidance. As I prayed, I understood: "Submission to my husband gives me freedom and maintains the divine order. *Obedience is better than sacrifice.*"

I realized that I'd been trying to earn a reward from the Lord through sacrifice when I should have been practicing obedience to the Scripture. It would have been easy for me to have gone without food, smugly feeling that I'd earned the right to make a request of God.

To give up and say "Yes, Pat" was harder on my ego—but remembering the scripture, that's what I did.

By doing our obedient best in whatever our place may be, we can glorify God and, at the same time, find more personal happiness than we can through stubborn opposition to authority.

In other words, a bank teller by working conscientiously can glorify God without endorsing every policy set by the bank's directors. Judgment of the policies and of the directors is up to God, not up to the teller. Our position should be to pray for them. [1]

Of course, should an employer order an employee to commit a crime or an indisputably immoral act, the employee should refuse. But this would be an exceptional situation.

A woman worked in our home for a time who was a sincere Christian but who could not adjust to our ideas of her position as cook. Despite her many fine qualities, she persistently involved herself in family conversations and affairs until our relationship became, to put it mildly, strained. If I didn't talk with her about any and everything at the greatest length, her feelings were hurt. Or, if I did try to talk with her about something, she misunderstood and another upset followed. She decided I didn't like black people.

But, if I know my own heart, that's not one of my hang-ups, and I assured her that was *not* the source of our problems. Our communication became so bad that I finally gave up trying to communicate with her at all and left it entirely up to Pat.

This wasn't satisfactory either; so after six months of misunderstandings on both sides, we let her go.

Thus the Lord had put me back into the kitchen, a place I hadn't been in for quite a while, but where I rediscovered the satisfaction of cooking for my family. I'm still enjoying it many months later!

Meanwhile, though, our former cook called for a job reference and, since she hadn't found employment, I asked her if she'd like to work two days for us while we were getting ready to go on tour. She said she would.

Because our relationship had been strained, I asked God to improve it, and it seemed to me that He instructed me to pray with her. Therefore, the second day that she was working for us, I suggested that we go to her room for prayer.

She welcomed the idea, so she, Cherry and I prayed together. Then, still trying to follow the guidance of God, I explained to her as gently as I could exactly what she'd done that bothered us while she was with us.

I told her, "The servant shouldn't work for the employer as much as for the Lord. When you find the place the Lord intends you to fill, He can use you for His glory in whatever home it may be." [2]

After that, I felt another urging from God—that I humble myself and wash her feet! I felt impressed that she was part of the body of Christ and that we are to subject ourselves one to another, and also that we are in honor to prefer one another, showing affection and brotherly love. [3]

Yes, the idea was unusual, but, obedient to what I felt was His word, I read the scripture passage about foot-washing (John 13:3-17) and then asked, "May I wash your feet and pray over you?"

She may have been startled, but she didn't object. So I washed her feet. We began praying and, as we did, she began to speak in her new language!

Though she'd long been a devout Christian, she hadn't previously received the baptism of the Holy Spirit. But, as we knelt together, she was blessed with her own Pentecost.

Needless to say, Cherry and I were blessed by sharing her new experience with the Lord! Now I'm sure that, wherever she works in the future, she'll be happier. So will her employers! She may *even* work for us again! Filled with the Spirit, she'll work not for people—but for the glory of the Lord.

My belief is that we are each happiest when we serve God in our appointed place, being submissive to the authority over us. However, I'm not condemning ambition or a desire for advancement. Jesus, in the parable about the talents, praised initiative.

I just know that if we each concentrate on our individual relationships with the Lord and not upon the shortcomings of those over us—or the "bad deal" we got—God will deal with every layer of authority according to His will, so that blessings will come to all who trust Him.

I've seen that only in God's divine order is there real freedom.

"Free as a bird . . ." Yes, the bird *is* free—free to obey God's natural laws and to accept His loving provision. And the bird joyfully wings through the sky—obeying God the whole time!

This is what "one woman's liberation" is all about—I'm free as a bird!

FOOTNOTES

Preface

1. "The thief comes only to steal, and kill, and destroy; I came that they might have life, and might have it abundantly." John 10:10

Chapter 4

1. "And we know that God causes all things to work together for good to those who love God, to those who are called according to His purpose." Romans 8:28

Chapter 9

1. Read Mark 14:3-9.
2. "Or do you not know that your body is a temple of the Holy Spirit who is in you, whom you have from God, and that you are not your own?" 1 Corinthians 6:19

Chapter 12

1. Read Matthew 28:18-20; Mark 16:15-18; John 14:16-21, and 1 Timothy 1:7
2. "And these signs will accompany those who have believed: in My name they will cast out demons, they will speak with new tongues." Mark 16:17
3. "And they went out and preached everywhere, while the Lord worked with them, and confirmed the word by the signs that followed." Mark 16:20

Chapter 13

1. Read Luke 11:5-13.
2. "The Spirit Himself bears witness with our Spirit that we are children of God." Romans 8:16

Chapter 15

1. "For the gifts and the calling of God are irrevocable." Romans 11:29
2. "But one and the same Spirit works all these things, distributing to each one individually just as He wills." 1 Corinthians 12:11

3. "Be still and know that I am God." Psalm 46:10, RSV
4. "And we know that God causes all things to work together for good to those who love God, to those who are called according to His purpose." Romans 8:28
5. "The heart is more deceitful than all else and is desperately sick: Who can understand it?" Jeremiah 17:9

Chapter 16

1. "The wind blows where it wishes and you hear the sound of it, but do not know where it comes from and where it is going; so is every one who is born of the Spirit." John 3:8
2. "For truly I say to you, if you have faith as a mustard seed, you shall say to this mountain, 'Move from here to there,' and it shall move; and nothing shall be impossible to you." Matthew 17:20
3. "No temptation has overtaken you but such as is common to man; and God is faithful, who will not allow you to be tempted beyond what you are able; but with the temptation will provide the way of escape also that you may be able to endure it." 1 Corinthians 10:13

Chapter 17

1. "Rejoice in the Lord always; again I will say, rejoice!" Philippians 4:4
2. "Always giving thanks for all things in the name of our Lord Jesus Christ to God, even the Father." Ephesians 5:20
3. Read James 5:13-16.
4. Read Luke 4:38,39 and Mark 5:22-42
5. Read John 11:1-45.
"Jesus said to him, 'Have I been so long with you, and *yet* you have not come to know Me, Philip? He who has seen Me has seen the Father; how do you say, "Show us the Father"?' " John 14:9

Chapter 18

1. Read Matthew 5:1-12.
2. "Blessed are those who hunger and thirst for righteousness, for they shall be satisfied." Matthew 5:6
3. *"Then* the Lord knows how to rescue the godly from temptation, and to keep the unrighteous under punishment for the day of judgement." 2 Peter 2:9
4. "No temptation has overtaken you but such as is common to man; and God is faithful, who will not allow you to be tempted beyond what you are

able; but with the temptation will provide the way of escape also, that you may be able to endure it." 1 Corinthians 10:13

5. "Those whom I love, I reprove and discipline; be zealous therefore, and repent." Revalation 3:19

Chapter 22

1. "For our struggle is not against flesh and blood, but against the rulers, against the powers, against the world-forces of this darkness, against the spiritual forces of wickedness in the heavenly places." Ephesians 6:12

2. Read Deuteronomy 18:9-14.

3. Read Matthew 4:5,6.

4. Read Acts 12.

5. Read 1 Samuel 28.

6. Read Deuteronomy 18:10-12; Isaiah 47:10-15; Acts 19:19 and Ephesians 5:10.

7. "The thief comes only to steal, and kill, and destroy; I came that they might have life, and might have it abundantly." John 10:10

Chapter 23

1. Read 1 Timothy 6:12-14.

Chapter 24

1. Read Romans 13.

2. Read Ephesians 6:5-8.

"You younger men, likewise, be subject to your elders; and all of you, clothe yourselves with humility toward one another, for God is opposed to the proud, but gives grace to the humble." 1 Peter 5:5

3. "Be devoted to one another in brotherly love; give preference to one another in honor." Romans 12:10

All Scripture is taken from the *New American Standard Bible,* unless otherwise noted.